C0-AWT-582

New Venture Performance

New Venture Performance

The Role of Strategy and Industry Structure

William R. Sandberg
University of Houston

Lexington Books
D.C. Heath and Company/Lexington, Massachusetts/Toronto

Library of Congress Cataloging-in-Publication Data

Sandberg, William R., 1949–
New venture performance.

Bibliography: p.
Includes index.
1. New business enterprises. 2. Entrepreneur. 3. Venture capital. 4. Efficiency, Industrial.
I. Title.
HD62.5.S27 1986 658.4'2 85-40193
ISBN 0-669-10919-3 (alk. paper)

Published simultaneously in Canada
Printed in the United States of America on acid-free paper
International Standard Book Number: 0-669-10919-3
Library of Congress Catalog Card Number: 85-40193

The paper used in this publication meets the minimum requirements of American National Standard for Information Sciences—Permanence of Paper for Printed Library Materials, ANSI Z39.48-1984.

The last numbers on the right below indicate the number and date of printing.

10 9 8 7 6 5 4 3 2 1

95 94 93 92 91 90 89 88 87 86

To Elaine, my wife, in appreciation of her love and unwavering support.

Contents

Figure and Tables

Figure

Tables

Acknowledgments

My research would have been impossible without the cooperation and assistance of many people. Noteworthy among them were the venture capitalists whom I interviewed or who permitted me to peruse their files of venture proposals. Only their necessary anonymity prevents my thanking them by name. I am also grateful to David Schweiger, Jon Goodman, and Jim Sowers, colleagues at the University of Houston, and Phyllis Holland of Georgia State University for their various forms of assistance.

I am especially indebted to Charles Hofer, my major professor and dissertation chair at the University of Georgia, who has served as my strategic management teacher ever since I was a student in his M.B.A. business policy course at Northwestern University in 1972. I have benefited immensely from our relationship and hope that Chuck will derive some satisfaction from seeing the results of his teaching.

Thanks are due also to the International Council for Small Business, whose dissertation proposal competition provided financial assistance to my work. Finally, I am grateful to Mr. E. F. Heizer, Jr., for supporting the new venture research award given by the Business Policy and Planning Division of the Academy of Management. The Heizer Award encourages and spotlights young researchers in the emerging field of entrepreneurship.

1
New Venture Performance as a Strategic Issue

This book focuses on independent new ventures that are intended to become substantial enterprises rather than mere sources of employment for an owner. It investigates the factors that contribute to the success or failure of such ventures and their entrepreneurs.

Entrepreneurship has become a hot subject in the 1980s. The business press has discovered it; *Venture* and *Inc.* magazines not only cover but exemplify entrepreneurship, and the *Wall Street Journal, Fortune,* and *Business Week* have devoted more attention to it. Popular business authors have embraced entrepreneurship—indirectly through renewed interest in high-profile "leadership," and directly through a spate of books dedicated to entrepreneurship and its practitioners.[1] There also has been a surge in the number of universities offering courses in entrepreneurship and in the number of professors showing an interest in teaching such courses and researching entrepreneurship topics.

Early on it became apparent to me that, despite all this attention, there was little progress toward understanding and prescribing solutions for the performance problems that seem to plague new ventures. As will be seen in later chapters, researchers lacked even a conceptual framework with which to examine new venture performance, although the elements of such a framework had been suggested. Venture capitalists, on the other hand, used some basic criteria and decision rules in evaluating proposed ventures and seemed to be rather successful in choosing likely winners.

In my research I set out with the ideas that new ventures might be treated as a special case of existing strategic management theory and that venture capitalists might be a source of conceptual guidance. Essentially, the objectives of this research were to develop a new conceptual model (or framework) and to test propositions concerning new venture performance. The new conceptual framework presents new venture performance as a result of the concatenation of strategy, industry structure, and the entrepreneur.

In chapter 1, I discuss the importance of new ventures and the difficulty of understanding what determines their performance. Some analysts attribute venture capitalists' success in selecting promising new ventures to their evaluation criteria. These criteria turn out to be the same factors examined by researchers in economics, entrepreneurship, and strategic management. Thus venture capitalists' success points to the potential value of a conceptual framework that integrates these areas to explain new venture performance.

With the genesis and rationale of this research established, the balance of the chapter describes its objectives, focus, and potential contribution. Chapter 1 concludes with a chapter-by-chapter outline of the book.

The Importance of New Ventures

New businesses are credited with playing a major role in the economic and social betterment of the United States. Karl H. Vesper recently undertook to enumerate and elaborate on the economic, personal, and social aspects of entrepreneurial activity. In his opinion, "entrepreneurship, the creation of new independent businesses, is an important national resource." Indeed, Vesper has concisely stated the case for new businesses:

> New businesses add products and services that improve choices for consumers and build competitive strengths for the nation against foreign rivals. Entrepreneurial ventures provide a competitive spur to existing companies, both large and small, stimulating them to improve quality and reduce price to the benefit of buyers. They accelerate the advance and dissemination of new technologies which enhance national defense and the quality of life at the same time. The new jobs they create provide more alternatives for employment, particularly for many individuals who have difficulty finding or fitting into the rigid slots of established organizations. New ventures are territory essential for the pursuit of happiness by many. Through entrepreneurship more people become leaders and economic power becomes more decentralized, broadening the base for a democratic economy.[2]

To their partisans, then, and to other researchers as well, new businesses (or startups) play a key economic role and ought to be regarded as a major source of the social mobility that is vital to a dynamic, free society.[3] The importance of new ventures can also be gauged in terms of the amounts invested in them. Although the total investment of capital and time in new and very young businesses is unknown, an estimated $30 billion was invested in 1983 alone.[4]

The Small Business Administration (SBA) encourages this investment by providing funds to leverage private equity raised by over 300 Small Business Investment Corporations (SBICs). In 1983 SBICs had about $1.6 billion in capital, roughly half of it from government loans. By contrast, private venture capital groups raised $4.5 billion in 1983 and $4.0 billion in 1984; the 100 largest invested $2.33 billion in 1983 and $2.28 billion in 1984.[5]

A substantial minority of both SBA loans and private venture capital has been placed in new ventures. The SBA reports that about 30 percent of its loans are to new businesses. Venture capitalists for several years had invested nearly 30 percent of their funds in startups, although that figure fell to 21 percent in 1984. Despite the lower percentage, venture capitalists invested more in startups in 1984 than in 1980.[6]

From the standpoint of the economic and social contributions claimed on behalf of new businesses, investments in startups may be the most important of the SBA and venture capital commitments. For many people the process of social mobility begins with the initiation of a new business. The process also ends here, at least temporarily, for many entrepreneurs. The failure rate among new ventures, although not known with certainty, is regarded as extremely high. Estimates vary, and some dispute the high mortality rate, but academics' most common estimate is said to be 65 percent failure by the fifth year after startup.[7]

Whatever the true rate of new venture failure, it represents a sizable loss in funds and opportunity. There is an obvious stake and potential profit in understanding why new ventures fail, why they succeed, and how their performance can be improved.

Understanding New Venture Performance

The challenge of understanding new venture performance has been approached from widely different perspectives by economists, entrepreneurship researchers, strategic management researchers, and other academic investigators. Nevertheless, new venture performance remains largely unexplained by each of these groups.

The same topic has also been approached by authors in the business and popular presses. Most of them believe that new venture performance is partially controllable by the entrepreneur. Many offer advice, and some report dramatically improved performance on the part of those entrepreneurs who heed their advice, follow their procedures, or meet certain criteria.

Evaluating Proposed New Ventures

Venture capitalists are among the most conspicuous—and conspicuously successful—new venture investors. The failure rate among their ventures is reportedly very low. Dorsey found an 18-percent failure rate within seven years of startup among 272 ventures funded by 77 venture capitalists, and White contrasted an alleged 80-percent, three-year failure rate for new ventures with the 8-percent, five-year failure rate among those backed by a large bank's SBIC.[8] White credited the difference to the SBIC's rigorous selection criteria.

Part of the explanation for this low failure rate may lie in the differences between the overall population of new ventures and those that seek venture capital. It may be that seekers of venture capital are a different and generally superior breed of entrepreneur. Even this cannot account for the entire difference, however, since Bruno and Tyebjee found a 30-percent failure rate among 193 ventures that had been rejected by at least one venture capitalist.[9] Over 40 percent of their sample were at least three years old at the time they sought funding, which suggests they had survived at least the early hazards that claim many startups. This increases the contrast between the sample's 30-percent, two-year (or less) failure rate and the 18-percent, seven-year failure rate that Dorsey reported for startups receiving venture capital. Evidently the venture capitalists' criteria are of some value.

As will be seen in chapter 2, venture capitalists rely on diverse, frequently subjective criteria in evaluating ventures. Some criteria reflect the interests or limitations of the venture capitalist rather than any shortcoming of a venture, but most rejections are based on the venture's management, its business plan, or its financial structure and prospects.[10] The same factors, broadly construed, are examined by the academic researchers in strategic management, entrepreneurship, and economics. If these researchers have not succeeded in predicting new venture performance, while venture capitalists have used the same factors to develop a fairly effective evaluation process, perhaps the explanation can be found in the failure of the academic researchers to integrate each other's insights, theories, and methods.

Venture capitalists' criteria may themselves be a promising research issue. At this point, though, it seems premature to focus primarily on those criteria. Instead my research focuses on developing a theory of new venture performance on which future inquiries could be based. Once in possession of an integrated conceptual framework, a researcher would be better equipped to identify and assess venture capitalists' criteria for new venture evaluation.

The research task at this stage in the development of a theory of new venture performance is to draw on selected academic fields to develop a conceptual framework. This framework would provide a way to view and understand data on new ventures and their performance, thereby permitting analysis and testing of relationships among key variables that might explain new venture performance.

Contributions and Limitations of Academic Literature

The distinct fields of economics, entrepreneurship research, and strategic management have contributed to the literature on new venture performance. Table 1–1 highlights the contribution of each field.

Table 1–1
Summary of Research and Theory on Entrepreneurs and New Venture Performance

Economists

The entrepreneur confronts an uncertain future that he views differently from others, and acts on that view.

If successful, the entrepreneur moves the economy toward (not away from) equilibrium; the entrepreneur's activities are bound up in the differences in knowledge, ignorance, and error in an economy in disequilibrium.

Strategic Management

A firm's strategy affects its performance.

Strategies are more desirable if they create or exploit asymmetries among firms and contexts (i.e., disequilibrium).

Entry is more attractive when an industry is significantly in disequilibrium.

Entrepreneurship

Entrepreneurial performance is *not* clearly related to the entrepreneur's need for achievement, locus of control, risk preference, education, or nonconformity.

Entrepreneurial success *is* associated with experience in startups and/or in a similar line of business.

Among economists, the so-called Austrian school has provided the key insights into the role and reasoning of the entrepreneur. Essentially, Austrians conceive of an entrepreneur who acts upon a dissenting view of the future, and whose actions succeed by driving a disequilibrated market toward equilibrium.[11] Other economists have not generally adopted the Austrian view of the entrepreneur. Disequilibrium at the industry or market level has been the domain of industrial organization economists, whose industry-level frame of reference and econometric research methods have usually overlooked the entrepreneur—and indeed the firm—as a unit of analysis.

A substantial literature on entrepreneurship does exist, although it has more in common with psychology than with economics or strategic management research. Although they have looked at the individual and attempted to explain what makes someone a successful entrepreneur, these studies have not established a causal relationship between psychological variables and new venture performance.[12] Entrepreneurial success *has* been related to experience, though.[13] This suggests a process of learning—about one's self, an industry, or entrepreneurship in general—that aids an entrepreneur. The implication is that many different types of entrepreneur can succeed, depending on their knowledge and skill in areas that are particularly important in their line of business.

Strategic management research has not focused on new venture performance. Its theory and research have established links between strategy and performance for declining businesses, low-share businesses, turnaround situations, and under other conditions—but not for new ventures.[14] The stumbling blocks confronting new venture researchers seem familiar to the strategic management researcher: lack of a theoretical framework; lack of clear, generic strategies; lack of an adequate data base for highly quantitative research; and the often prohibitive difficulty, time, and expense of securing adequate case data for using traditional business policy research methods on new ventures.

Even so, strategic management can contribute several things to the study of new venture performance. Most important is an understanding of strategy and of its effects on performance. The unifying trait of the strategic management research cited above is the key role played by strategy. In each situation, certain strategies proved more effective than others. Furthermore, some strategic management researchers and theorists have made explicit the strategic desirability of creating or exploiting "asymmetries" (or disequilibrium).[15] This becomes more clear in the integrative work of Yip, who examined the effects of both industry structure and entry strategies on the likelihood of entry and the performance of industry entrants.[16]

Objective and Focus of the Book

Although the academic fields described above have not produced a theory of new venture performance, they have developed concepts and theories that could contribute to such a theory. Venture capitalists have experienced success in evaluating new ventures and appear to rely on criteria that emphasize the caliber of the entrepreneur, the venture's strategy, and the nature of the industry to be entered.

Despite their success in screening out failures, one should not assume that the venture capitalists' criteria produce optimal decisions or forecasts of venture performance. Obviously, some failures are backed; but some winners probably are overlooked, too, if most of Bruno and Tyebjee's sample survived.[17]

Thus it may be possible to build on the venture capitalists' criteria by adding concepts and techniques from the academic world to those criteria. And it seems possible to advance the state of knowledge and theory concerning new venture performance by drawing on successful practitioners and by integrating the work of the disparate academic fields that address the topic.

This book undertakes such an integration. It draws on both academic research (in strategic management, economics, and entrepreneurship) and practitioner wisdom (gleaned from both literature and interviews with five venture capital practitioners) to develop a conceptual framework of new venture performance.

This book departs significantly from traditional research and theory in entrepreneurship, which has generally assumed that new venture performance is a function of the characteristics of the entrepreneur, or $NVP = f(E)$.

The framework developed here draws from the wisdom of venture capitalists, whose criteria suggest the following, more complete model: $NVP = f(E, IS, S)$, or that new venture performance is a function of the characteristics of the entrepreneur, the structure of the industry being entered, and the venture strategy.

My research required a synthesis of theory and knowledge from entrepreneurship, economics, and strategic management to capture the determinants of new venture performance. On the basis of that synthesis, I developed and tested nineteen propositions relating to new venture performance and, more specifically, to seven research questions. The objective was to investigate the following research issues:

1. How much and in what ways a new venture's strategy affects its performance.
2. How much and in what ways industry structure affects a new venture's performance.
3. How much and in what ways an entrepreneur's track record and other characteristics affect a new venture's performance.
4. The effects of venture strategy, industry structure, and an entrepreneur's experience and characteristics when taken in combination.

Each issue was examined through an analysis of original data on a sample of seventeen new ventures that sought venture capital funding between 1974 and 1982. Several points set this research apart from prior investigations of these issues.

First, very few if any prior studies of independent (that is, not corporate-sponsored) new ventures have attempted integrative work in the theory and the research issues addressed here. Prior conceptual and theoretical work has rarely noted, and more rarely researched, the combined effects of venture strategy, industry structure, and an entrepreneur's characteristics. These are the focus of my research.

Second, venture strategy is classified according to two theory-based schemes that have been used to develop and test theory in strategic management. This permits the researcher to draw on more mature related fields to advance research in his own.

Third, the study includes preliminary field interviews with venture capitalists, whose financial success depends on their ability to predict new venture performance. The research issues combine the overlapping perspectives of academics and practitioners, based in part on these interviews.

Fourth, the principal source of data is the proposal submitted by the entrepreneur to the venture capitalist. Rather than neglecting strategy (as most studies have done), or inferring it from actions taken over succeeding years, or relying on after-the-fact recountings of what was intended and done during the venture's early years, this research captures strategy as it was stated for the record in the venture's early years.

Fifth, the data base includes failed as well as successful ventures. Some received funds but failed; others were unable to obtain funds from the venture capitalists who participated in this research. Many studies have examined only surviving ventures or successful entrepreneurs.

Outline of the Book

Chapter 2 covers the issues of new venture performance from the perspective of venture capitalists. Two methods are employed to identify the wisdom of venture capitalists. The first is a review of the literature on venture capitalists' investment decision criteria. The second is a series of five interviews with practitioners in the venture capital business. They echo the industry's consensus on the importance of an entrepreneur's track record and on basic strategic and industry structural desiderata.

Chapter 3 is a review of the literature on new venture performance, entrepreneurship, and related topics. The argument is made that strategic management and industrial organization both offer important contributions to the study of new venture performance. This book makes use of both fields and of entrepreneurship research to identify and describe key factors that might affect new venture performance.

Chapter 4 develops a conceptual framework of new venture performance and defines the terms, descriptions, and categories used in this research. As a first step, it presents an *academic framework* and a *practitioner framework* that were developed from the interviews and literature.

The new, synthesized conceptual framework combines the performance orientation of practitioners and the mapping and classification contributions of academics. It includes strategy and industry structure as independent variables that affect new venture performance and retains the characteristics of the entrepreneur that have been most closely related to venture performance. This combination of variables represents a new paradigm for new venture research.

Venture business strategy is conceived and detailed on the basis of the works of Hofer and Schendel, Abell, Porter, and Vesper.[18] Product–market scope, distinctive competence, and competitive advantage are the heart of the strategy, with attention also given to specific entry strategies and overall business definition strategies.

The new model accounts for industry structure primarily by identifying barriers and gateways to entry.[19] Product differentiation, a key factor in the framework, is viewed both as a barrier and as a gateway to entry. The framework follows both economists and strategic management researchers in identifying disequilibrium as a vital aid to entrants.[20] It also adopts the theoretical claims of Abell concerning the proper business definition strategies for entry during early and late stages of industry evolution.[21]

The entrepreneur's characteristics that appear in the model include prior entrepreneurial and startup experience, managerial experience in related industries, age, and education. Both academic and venture capital experts have identified these as keys to entrepreneurial performance.

New venture performance is conceived in terms of profitability and survival. Ventures are divided into highly successful, successful, marginal, unsuccessful, and highly unsuccessful categories.

Seven research questions and 19 propositions are presented in the latter portion of chapter 4. They deal with venture business strategy, industry structure, and the entrepreneur's characteristics separately, then in pairs, and finally in a three-way combination.

Chapter 5 describes the methodology of my research. Because it is exploratory, theory-building research, its objective is to develop and test an understanding of what determines new venture performance. To achieve both richness of detail and broader generalizability, I developed 17 case studies of new ventures, collected longitudinal performance data, and performed statistical tests on the data.

No prior research has subjected new venture strategy–industry structure relationships to statistical tests. Moreover, the literature review uncovered no prior use of case data in conjunction with statistical tests of new venture strategy or of industry structure and entry (whether by new ventures alone or by all entrants).

Chapter 5 also describes the procedure by which the data were gathered and analyzed. Seventeen new ventures were selected from the files of participating venture capitalists. Information from the venture business plans was used to classify each venture's strategy, industry structure, and entrepreneur. Only after completing these classifications did I seek performance information—and then only from the venture capitalist or the public record, never from the entrepreneur or venture. The chapter concludes by discussing the statistical tests to be used and the reasons for this selection.

Chapter 6 presents and analyzes the results. Venture performance was compared among categories of strategy, industry structure, and entrepreneur. The propositions concerning business strategy and/or industry structure effects were tested with the Mann–Whitney U Test. All propositions which included the entrepreneur's characteristics were tested with the Spearman rank correlation. I have interpreted the strength of demonstrated relationships and identified areas in which potentially valuable information could not be captured and tested until theory and research were more fully developed. On the basis of these findings, chapter 6 offers prescriptions for venture business strategy that are contingent upon an industry's stage of evolution.

Chapter 7 discusses the implications of my research. Chief among them are the evident importance and the contingent nature of venture business strategy and industry structure in explaining and predicting new venture performance.

For both venture capitalists and entrepreneurs, this means that much of their current wisdom is confirmed but with some qualifications and exceptions. Most significantly, the findings call into question the value of niche-filling as opposed to broadly defined, differentiated strategies.

These findings have several implications for research. First, they suggest the validity of the new paradigm offered here: Strategy and industry structure have significant effects on new venture performance. Subsequent research should incorporate both factors. Their effects remain to be measured, however, which indicates a needed line of research. The chapter proposes several further steps and one specific research project to pursue a theory of new venture performance.

Second, this book makes methodological contributions. It indicates the superiority of Abell's over Porter's strategy classification scheme for new venture research and perhaps for strategy research in general.[22] It also shows the value of a common vocabulary and classification scheme for the conduct of new venture research.

Finally, this book shows that practitioners' unarticulated theories and frameworks can contribute to new venture research. Practitioner interviews helped point out areas of research on which to draw in synthesizing a new conceptual framework of new venture performance.

Notes

1. In addition to its regular small business column, the *Wall Street Journal* has published a 112-page special report on small business (Section 3, May 20, 1985). The more prominent recent books include Peter F. Drucker, *Innovation and Entrepreneurship: Practice and Principles* (New York: Harper & Row, 1985) and George Gilder, *The Spirit of Enterprise* (New York: Simon and Schuster, 1984).

2. Karl H. Vesper, *Entrepreneurship and National Policy* (Chicago: Heller Institute for Small Business Policy, 1983), p. 6.

3. Additional arguments, references, and data on the importance of entrepreneurship can be found in Vesper, *Entrepreneurship and National Policy.*

4. Gail Gregg, "Investing in Entrepreneurs," *Venture* 6 (June 1984):46–50.

5. These data come from industry coverage by Udayan Gupta ("SBICs," *Ven-*

ture 5 [October 1983]:66-68) and Michele H. Fleischer ("The Venture Capital 100: Caution is the Word," *Venture* 7 [June 1985]:48–56).

6. Fleischer, "The Venture Capital 100."

7. Albert Shapero, "Numbers That Lie," *Inc.* 3 (May 1981):16–18.

8. Terry Dorsey, *Operating Guidelines for Effective Venture Capital Funds Management* (Austin: The University of Texas, 1979); Richard White, *The Entrepreneur's Manual* (Radnor, Pa.: Chilton, 1977).

9. Albert V. Bruno and Tyzoon T. Tyebjee, "The One That Got Away: A Study of Ventures Rejected by Venture Capitalists," in *Frontiers of Entrepreneurship Research*, (edited by John A. Hornaday, Jeffry A. Timmons, and Karl H. Vesper, (Wellesley, Mass.: Babson College Center for Entrepreneurial Studies, 1983), pp. 289–306.

10. James M. Johnson, "Determinants of Unsuccessful Risk Capital Funding by Small Business," *American Journal of Small Business* 4 (July 1979):31–38.

11. Austrian economics is traced to Carl Menger. Its fundamentals are set out in Menger's *Principles of Economics,* an 1871 work available in translation (New York: New York University Press, 1981). The major Austrian treatise is by Ludwig von Mises (*Human Action,* 3rd rev. ed., Chicago: Henry Regnery Company, 1966). The leading modern Austrian economist is Israel Kirzner of New York University, author of *Perception, Opportunity, and Profit* (Chicago: University of Chicago Press, 1979). The Austrian view of entrepreneurship is summarized by Dolores Tremewan Martin, "Alternative Views of Mengerian Entrepreneurship," *History of Political Economy* 11 (1979):271–285.

12. Robert H. Brockhaus, "Psychological and Environmental Factors Which Distinguish the Successful from the Unsuccessful Entrepreneur: A Longitudinal Study," *Proceedings, Academy of Management,* 1980:368–372; also Robert H. Brockhaus, "Psychology of the Entrepreneur," a paper presented at the Conference on Research and Education in Entrepreneurship, St. Louis University, March, 1980; and Robert H. Brockhaus, "Risk-Taking Propensity of Entrepreneurs," *Academy of Management Journal* 23 (1980):509–520.

13. Orvis F. Collins and David G. Moore, *The Enterprising Man* (MSU Business Studies, 1964; Bureau of Business and Economic Research; Graduate School of Business Administration; Michigan State University. East Lansing, Mich.: Michigan State University, 1964); William M. Hoad and Peter Rosko, *Management Factors Contributing to the Success and Failure of New Small Manufacturers* (Ann Arbor, Mich.: Bureau of Business Research, University of Michigan, 1964).

14. Kathryn Rudie Harrigan, *Strategies for Declining Businesses* (Lexington, Mass.: Lexington Books, 1980); Carolyn Y. Y. Woo, "Strategies for Low Market Share Businesses," Ph.D. diss., Purdue University, West Lafayette, Ind. 1980; Charles W. Hofer, "Turnaround Strategies," *Journal of Business Strategy* 1 (Summer 1980):19–31.

15. Richard Rumelt, "Evaluation of Strategy: Theory and Models," in *Strategic Management,* (edited by Dan E. Schendel and Charles W. Hofer, Boston: Little, Brown, 1979), pp. 196–212.

16. George S. Yip, *Barriers to Entry: A Corporate-Strategy Perspective* (Lexington, Mass.: Lexington Books, 1982).

17. Bruno and Tyebjee, "The One That Got Away."

18. Charles W. Hofer and Dan E. Schendel, *Strategy Formulation: Analytical Concepts* (St. Paul, Minn.: West Publishing Co., 1978); Derek F. Abell, *Defining the Business: The Starting Point of Strategic Planning* (Englewood Cliffs, N.J.: Prentice-Hall, 1980); Michael E. Porter, *Competitive Strategy* (New York: Free Press, 1980); Karl H. Vesper, *New Venture Strategies* (Englewood Cliffs, N.J.: Prentice-Hall, 1980).

19. Porter, *Competitive Strategy;* Yip, *Barriers to Entry.*

20. Rumelt, "Evaluation of Strategy"; Yip, *Barriers to Entry.*

21. Abell, *Defining the Business.*

22. Ibid.; Porter, *Competitive Strategy.*

2
Venture Capitalists' Wisdom and Practices with Respect to New Ventures

Chapter 1 noted that the selectivity of venture capitalists may account for the comparatively low rate of failure among the ventures in which they invest. Venture capitalists' selectivity is reflected in the evaluation criteria they apply to proposed ventures.

What are the thoughts and practices of venture capitalists with respect to entrepreneurship and new ventures? Why are their investees more successful than the average new venture? In this chapter I begin to answer these questions by summarizing the evaluation criteria used by venture capitalists. These criteria emphasize the entrepreneur's characteristics and the venture's business plan.

Next I describe a sample of venture capitalists who were interviewed for this book. Their own thoughts and practices are similar to what prior studies have reported about venture capitalists. This similarity is important because several of these venture capitalists also provide sample ventures for this book. The chapter concludes with a summary statement of the extent of the venture capitalist's focus on the entrepreneur and venture business strategy in evaluating new ventures.

Reasons for Venture Capitalists' Success

The superior performance of ventures backed by venture capitalists could be attributed to several financial and nonfinancial factors besides the venture capitalists' selectivity. Several venture capitalists and consultants have written about them. Their views are described and discussed below.

The most obvious contribution of a venture capitalist to a new venture is the early infusion of equity capital. Since inadequate capitalization often is offered as an explanation for the failure of new or small firms, one could argue that venture capitalists increase the likelihood of new venture survival and success simply by providing capital. The research record is mixed; some studies have found a positive relationship between initial capitalization and the likelihood of venture success, but others have found different explanations for venture survival or failure. Vesper has commented, "In each of the failures additional capital could presumably have extended survival, but never was it clear that more capital would have allowed success."[1] A veteran SBIC president was still more emphatic: "And believe me when I say that *no small business ever failed because of a lack of funds.*"[2] He considered failure to be a symptom of poor wisdom and discipline in the company's commitment of funds.

A related financial benefit may be the venture capitalists' ability to provide subsequent rounds of financing. Allen considered this a major contribution but cautioned entrepreneurs that not all venture capitalists could or would fill this role. He pointed out that such financing often could be obtained from other sources, but at too great a dilution of the founder's equity position.[3] It should be noted that the disadvantage falls on the founder and not the venture in such situations.

The venture capitalist also is said to provide nonfinancial assistance and advice to investees.[4] The scope of this role is suggested by venture capital consultant Norman Fast. "They often become involved in planning and strategy development, assisting in recruiting for key positions and in developing relationships with important suppliers or customers."[5]

Despite the value of adequate capitalization and management help to the new venture, it does not seem likely that the venture capitalist's provision of them is decisive in determining which new ventures succeed and which fail. There are two principal reasons for this conclusion. First, both capital and management counsel are widely available in competitive markets. Presumably a venture or young company can secure what it needs of each without the help of a venture capitalist. Neither comes free, of course, but the venture capitalist does not provide capital or counsel on that basis either. A venture capitalist that offers valuable assistance probably wins more attractive terms in its investment agreements than one that provides nothing more than financing. A venture founder could elect to finance the venture through the latter type of venture capitalist and to provide equity participation to a consultant or other outside source of assistance.

Second, if the venture capitalist's advice and services accounted for a substantial part of the variance in venture performance, one would expect venture capitalists to devote most of their efforts to providing such services and rather little to screening ventures for investment. The fact that venture capitalists continue to screen proposals and to invest very selectively demonstrates that they believe certain characteristics are associated with likely successes. In 1985 industry analysts have noted that many venture capitalists lack the capacity and skills to meet their investees' increasing need for advice.[6]

Further evidence that capitalization and management assistance are not the keys to separating successful from unsuccessful ventures can be found by comparing the performance of venture capitalists to that of Community Development Corporations (CDCs), which use federally granted funds "to make venture capital type investments" and to provide follow-on financing, consulting, and other support to their portfolio companies.[7] CDC staff have prior experience in venture capital, consulting, or investment banking, and their services are offered at little or no cost to client firms. Even so, a 1978 review of the performance of CDCs revealed that 77 percent of their investees had failed or were unprofitable.

It may be that CDCs invest, for socio-political reasons, in less attractive prospects than do venture capitalists. But the CDCs purport to offer their clients a full range of financial and management services (the latter usually at no charge) of the type usually provided by venture capitalists. If these were indeed the critical determinants of new venture performance, one would expect CDC-backed ventures to perform more or less as do those backed by venture capitalists.

It is at this point in the argument that the selectivity of venture capitalists comes back into play. According to Fast, "The 125–150 leading venture capital firms screen tens of thousands of opportunities in a year to identify those 600–800 companies a year that have the greatest potential."[8] The fact that venture capitalists devote considerable resources to evaluating investment opportunities supports the inference that differences among ventures are important determinants of their performance. The fact that CDCs use criteria that differ in key respects from those used by venture capitalists supports the inference that the ventures in the two groups' portfolios also differ. The additional fact that venture capitalists' portfolios substantially outperform those of CDCs (which likewise offer financial support and counsel to their investees) supports the inference that the differing selection criteria lead to differences between the types of ventures backed and hence to the differences in venture performance.

Since the criteria used by venture capitalists seem to aid in the selection of ventures that are better prospects, these criteria are a potential source of information about what determines new venture performance.

Venture Capitalists' Evaluation Criteria

Venture capitalists are a diverse group, and their new venture evaluation criteria reflect this diversity. These criteria frequently embody preferences based on a venture's stage of development, its location, its industry or technology, or the size of the investment required. Venture capitalists have been found to base 24 percent of their rejections on policies that reflect their own interests, knowledge, and so on. More useful to this book are the reasons for rejection that related directly to the applicant venture's prospects, which appear to account for three-fourths or more of rejections.[9]

The caliber and depth of a venture's management are the traditional focus of venture capitalists' evaluations. This focus obeys the oft-repeated maxim of pioneer venture capitalist George Doriot: "A grade-A man with a grade-B idea is better than a grade-B man with a grade-A idea." Some researchers have reported success in explaining entrepreneurial success through psychology in terms of need for achievement, rebelliousness, beliefs as to locus of control, the existence of role models, and other personal traits, but venture capitalists do not formally examine these facets of the entrepreneur's personality.

Venture capitalists instead rely on a much narrower range of personal characteristics, which they assess far more informally. It is possible that they are influenced in this practice by the weakness of the psychological studies, which usually examine already-successful entrepreneurs rather than novices and that focus on averages rather than individuals.[10] Or they may trust other, more readily obtained data instead of attempting psychological testing. Or it may be true that "venture capitalists often rely to a large extent on their intuition" in seeking entrepreneurs who display "iron will, dogged determination, enthusiasm, and resourcefulness."[11]

A representative expression of the venture capitalist's viewpoint was written by Dingee, Smollen, and Haslett.[12] The authors, three venture capitalists, considered the entrepreneur's commitment, motivation, and skills the most important factor in evaluating venture capital investment proposals. The skills of the venture's management team and the viability of the business idea were also important. Desirable entrepreneurial traits included drive and energy level, self-confidence, persistence in problem solving, realism in setting challenging goals, moderate risk preferences, learning from failure, openness to criticism, initiative and self-responsibility, and the internal setting of standards. They also sought entrepreneurs who would offer long-term involvement, who saw money as a measure of performance rather than as an end, and who made good use of resources.

Besides scrutinizing the entrepreneur, venture capitalists appear to be united in requiring a business plan. "Such a plan describes the way in which a proposed firm is supposed to compete and presumably reflects considerable thought."[13] The plans described by various authors comprise many of the elements of a business strategy: the size and structure of the industry and the market, the segment(s) of particular interest, plans for entry, unique features of the product or service, required investment, projected return on investors' equity, social/political/cultural forces to be exploited or reckoned with, control systems to be used, and so on.

The combined importance of the entrepreneur and the venture business strategy in venture capitalists' decisions is shown by Johnson.[14] In his study,

39 percent of rejections were because of management quality or experience and 11 percent because of the business plan. An additional 32 percent were because of finance, but the specific reasons included capitalization, past profits, future profits, and viability—all of which (except past profits, of course) are expected to be detailed in a new venture's business plan.

Venture capitalists have addressed the strategic decisions on scope, distinctive competence, and competitive advantage. For example, Dingee et al. stated that venture capitalists want answers to certain standard questions when they evaluate the viability of a proposed venture. They want to know, What will be sold to whom, and for what customer motivations? Why will customers buy from this venture rather than from its rivals? Who are the competitors, are they profitable, and how will this venture compete against them? Is this a growth industry? What is the potential market?[15]

Louis Allen drew on his years as a manager at an early SBIC to propose specific guidelines on how to get customers and how to select products for a new business. He shared the venture capital industry's emphasis on a venture's quality of management, calling it "the primary consideration in every favorable recommendation"[16] he had made to his SBIC superiors, but he believed that certain approaches to competition were also important.

Allen recommended selecting products that required little expenditure for R&D, engineering, or market development. The products should form a narrow line and should be targeted to customers whose needs can be met by a limited product line that is sold on some basis other than price. He urged entrepreneurs to seek small orders from numerous customers and to avoid reliance on a handful of buyers for a major proportion of sales.

Allen also believed the product should be one that is essential to its buyers, turns over quickly, is produced in short runs, is made exclusive through the application of production know-how, and requires the sort of intensive after-sales service that builds customer loyalty. It should be relatively immune to cyclical demand, innovation, or other types of change.

A. David Silver, a venture capitalist and writer who has since abandoned Manhattan for New Mexico, offered a somewhat different prescription.[17] He described eight factors that led to a venture's success. Most of the factors restated conventional wisdom from the venture capital industry (for example, the existence of a large number of buyers who needed and could afford the product, a lack of institutional barriers to selling or distributing it, the ability of the venture to remain "invisible" to incumbents or potential entrants), but one was a departure from convention. Silver identified *homogeneity of buyers* as an important factor, reasoning that if one solution suited the needs of many customers, the new venture would be spared additional investment as its market base expanded. Silver's "standard solution to a standard problem" partially contradicts Allen and others who prefer a narrower focus on customer types. It does not, however, require a broad product line.

In sum, venture capitalists agree that the quality of the entrepreneur is the primary issue in evaluating a proposed venture. They seem to be in accord on what to look for in an entrepreneur: "iron will, dogged determination, enthusiasm, and resourcefulness."[18] And most of them prefer a relatively narrow, specialized approach to product line and market segmentation choices. But specific advice remains atheoretical and appears to rely more on each writer's experience than on any articulated view of the new venture and its economic setting.

The most thorough empirical research on venture capitalists' criteria is a study by Tyebjee and Bruno, who administered a structured questionnaire to 41 venture capitalists. Through factor analysis they identified five evaluation criteria that together explained 60 percent of the variance in the venture capitalists' investment decisions. In order of importance, the criteria were (1) market attractiveness; (2) product differentiation; (3) managerial capabilities of the venture founders; (4) resistance to environmental threats; and (5) cash-out potential.[19]

Two aspects of Tyebjee and Bruno's findings stand out. First, they are consistent with other, less empirical descriptions of the criteria. Second, the essence of business strategy is captured in market attractiveness, product differentiation, and resistance to environmental threats. It would not be prudent to rely on Tyebjee and Bruno's criteria rankings, however, because of a flaw in their research design. The 41 respondents provided evaluations of 90 ventures, an average of 2.2 apiece. Thus the criteria weights of some venture capitalists were counted more heavily than those of others, simply by virtue of the number of venture evaluations they provided.

In conclusion, it is possible to establish the existence of venture capitalists' evaluation criteria and to argue strongly for their effectiveness, but it is less easy to pinpoint the actual criteria. Elements of strategy and industry structure join the characteristics of the entrepreneurs in these criteria. While the questions venture capitalists ask may be fairly standard, the responses they desire appear not to be so uniform. The literature is sparse, and it reveals no thorough, integrated explanation of new venture performance in the stated criteria of venture capitalists.

Interviews with Venture Capitalists

Because venture capitalists' judgments of an entrepreneur and a business plan are crucial to their investment decisions, it seemed desirable to gain personal familiarity with the process and criteria by which venture capitalists arrive at their judgments. The literature provided general answers to many questions about the criteria, as described above. As a second step, interviews were conducted in 1981 and early 1982 with four venture capitalists and one consulting engineer who assists ventures in obtaining venture capital. These interviews had multiple purposes. First, they would fill out the statistical and general portrait already developed. Second, they would provide a check on the representativeness of the venture capitalists from whom venture data would be obtained for use in my research. Since about half of the sample came from venture capitalists who were interviewed, the same data were available from them as from the interviewed venture capitalists who did not provide sample ventures. All were solicited to participate, so the nonparticipants allowed an informal check on respondent–nonrespondent differences.

I conducted the interviews in single sessions, typically lasting 90 minutes. The interviews were guided by an outline of prepared questions, and whenever possible, an advance copy of the outline was given to the venture capitalist.

These four venture capitalists and their portfolios are described in the following paragraphs. Then their "wisdom" is reported and compared with earlier findings from the literature.

Description of Venture Capitalists and Their Portfolios

Legal Organization

The four venture capitalists represented an investment banking firm, a private venture capital firm, a limited partnership under the aegis of an international securities firm, and an SBIC. The first three were constrained in their investment decisions by internal policies but were otherwise free to exercise their own judgment. The SBIC, by virtue of its federal licensing and subsidized capitalization, was subject to certain restrictions. It could invest no more than one-fifth of its paid-in capital in any company and was barred from taking a controlling interest in any of its portfolio companies. There were also net worth and net income maxima for companies eligible to receive SBIC backing. The consulting engineer faced no restrictions in working with ventures.

Size

The SBIC and the limited partnership both ranked in the fourth quartile of the 100 largest venture capitalists, based on funds invested in 1981.[20] The private firm was considerably less active than these two in 1981, but by midyear had amassed a portfolio of about the same size (8 ventures versus 8 and 12 ventures) and of greater value ($15–20 million versus $5–10 million) than the SBIC and the limited partnership. The investment banking firm's annual investment volume fell short of the top 100 but its portfolio was comparable in size and value to the others interviewed.

Another important size consideration is the limit on individual investments. The SBIC was legally restricted to $1.1 million in each portfolio company. The limited partnership had a limit of $1 million, whereas the private firm had a ceiling between $2 million and $3 million, and the investment banker handled deals up to about $2 million. The consulting engineer preferred ventures in the $2–5 million range.

The interviewed venture capitalists were larger than the average for their industry. Their individual investment limits exceeded the average limit of less than $750,000 found in a sample of 291 high technology venture capitalists. The SBIC and limited partnership averaged just under $500,000 per initial investment in 1981. By comparison, 15 of the 50 most active venture capitalists reported average initial investments no greater than $500,000. Only 8 of the 50 reported a maximum figure in excess of $3 million.[21]

Specialization

Three of the four interviewed venture capitalists specialized by industry or by stage of venture development. The limited partnership sought high-technology manufacturing startups that were still in a precommercialization stage. The investment banker, too, specialized in high-technology ventures, but also was quite interested in leveraged buyouts of established companies. The private firm invested mainly in startups and specialized in natural resources, particularly coal. This choice reflected the expertise of the firm's investors rather than the original background of the venture capitalist himself. The SBIC was described by its head as "nonspecialized and diversified" in its investments.

There was some regional specialization on the part of the four venture capitalists. Although three portfolios were national in scope, one was composed primarily of western and southwestern companies. Taken together, the portfolios covered all regions except for the Midwest and North Central states.

Portfolios

Three of the four venture capitalists provided summary data on their portfolios. (To preserve their anonymity, these data are presented only in aggregate form.) The three had 28 ventures in their portfolios, of which 13 had been startup investments. Five other investments represented the first institutional financing obtained by young firms. The 13 startups included 8 high-technology manufacturers, 4 natural resource companies, and 1 service company. The fourth venture capitalist (the investment banker) had backed both service and high-technology manufacturing startup ventures.

The 28 ventures in the three portfolios included 12 high-technology manufacturers, 4 other manufacturers, 7 service or wholesaling ventures, and 5 natural resource ventures.

Venture Capitalists' Wisdom

The views and practices of the five interview participants are presented below. The discussion covers the characteristics of the entrepreneur, the structure and evolution of the industry, and the venture business strategy.

Characteristics of the Entrepreneur

The interview participants reflected the conventional wisdom of their industry by placing the greatest emphasis on the quality of a new venture's management. As one phrased his view, echoing Georges Doriot's maxim quoted earlier in this chapter: "We will pursue a mediocre idea with very fine people; we will never pursue a great idea with mediocre people." Another called quality of management "the big hurdle" and said, "I look for three things: management, management, and managment." Under the general headings of "management" or "people" the venture capitalists placed both the personal attributes and the experience of the entrepreneur.

The interview participants offered ready lists of qualities they sought in an entrepreneur. One frequently volunteered quality was described variously as high energy, persistence, or initiative; another as resourcefulness, flexibility, or practicality. The venture capitalists mentioned cooperativeness more often than any other personal attribute, with one describing it as "the entrepreneur's being receptive to advice as well as to capital." One venture capitalist who takes an active managerial role in some of his investments expressed his preference for a "reliable plodder" over the more brilliant person who would "go off half-cocked."

The entrepreneur's experience weighed heavily in the venture capitalists' evaluations, too. One stated bluntly that he would not back someone who previously had failed as an entrepreneur, and another called such a record "a significant minus." None offered any comments minimizing the significance of prior failure; the others did not refer to failure at all.

While startup experience was of only minor importance to all of them, the venture capitalists strongly preferred that an entrepreneur have what one called "generic experience as an entrepreneur." This experience was more valuable if gained in a small company, according to several of them. One explained that he sought those "experienced in running a small company where the margin for error is smaller." Another observed tartly, "Venture capital is not to be used for tuition." Experience in a related business was desirable, thought most of the venture capitalists, but this was less important than entrepreneurial experience. One venture capitalist qualified his comment by saying that experienced management was particularly important in service businesses because of low capital requirements and easy entry by imitators.

The entrepreneur's education was not a major consideration in evaluating a venture. Perhaps this was because the venture capitalists rarely encountered an entrepreneur who lacked a college degree, as one suggested. He added that a technical degree would be virtually required for some ventures but that an M.B.A. was never required. Another, who dealt entirely in technology-related ventures, saw added credibility conferred by an appropriate degree. By and large, though, the venture capitalists did not consider education an important factor in their decisions. This seems to reflect the results of a certain pre-screening rather than a general truth about all entrepreneurship, since these venture capitalists were exposed almost exclusively to intendedly high-growth ventures. In high-technology fields, and presumably to some extent elsewhere, such ventures are more likely to be conceived by more highly educated persons.

The venture capitalists were evenly divided between personal characteristics and experience as the most important factor. There appeared to be no pattern to their preferences (in this admittedly small sample), as neither size, nor relative exposure in new ventures, nor even the venture capitalist's degree of involvement in venture management explained their priorities.

Despite the importance of the personal characteristics just discussed, the venture capitalists used no formal, psychological tests or measurements to assess what one called "the amalgam of qualities" they considered. Even those who placed experience first relied on their own feel for the quality of an entrepreneur in the absence of a track record. The venture capitalists sometimes relied on references, especially from respected venture capital colleagues, to verify what they sensed.

Industry Structure and Evolution

The interviewed venture capitalists all had preferences concerning the types of industry in which they would invest. Some of their preferences were described above in discussing their specialization. Those preferences grew out of the venture capitalists' expertise, regional constraints, or other considerations that reflected the resources or limitations of the investor more so than of the venture. These venture capitalists expressed other industry-related preferences, however, that reflected their assessments of likely venture performance. These preferences focused on industry structure and evolution.

The interview participants preferred industries that were fragmented and still growing. This preference conforms to one's expectations based on the literature on venture capitalists. A specialist in high-tech new ventures offered this advice: "Avoid concentrated industries unless you can differentiate your product or there's a technological change." Another high-tech specialist shared this willingness to bet on a new product's overcoming stable, mature market conditions. The most diversified, nonspecialized venture capitalist, whose portfolio leaned more toward later-round or buyout financing, was willing to back an entrant in what he termed a "crowded industry" so long as differentiation and niche-filling were possible.

One venture capitalist's statements and deeds provided an informative contrast. Although he preferred fragmented, pre-maturity industries, this venture capitalist had invested in coal mining ventures. While fragmented, the coal mining industry certainly was not pre-maturity. The investments had been made during the mid-1970s' rapid rise in coal prices and demand, when the venture capitalist expected sustained growth and profits in a previously petrified industry. To this investor, at least, prospects for growth outweighed industry maturity in evaluating individual ventures.

Venture Business Strategy

All of the interviewed venture capitalists paid careful attention to a venture's business strategy. Each had his own terminology and adages with which to express his criteria for evaluating strategy, but the venture capitalists' criteria had a common core.

The unifying theme throughout the criteria was competitive advantage. One called it "differential advantage," another "compelling difference," but all sought it in a venture business strategy. The preferred origin of competitive advantages differed mainly according to the venture capitalist's orientation toward technology. High-tech specialists primarily thought in terms of proprietary product or process innovations. The more diversified venture capitalists usually were receptive to new technologies, to be sure, but were at least equally open to market-based strategies. Positioning in a niche or segment was their aim, and at least one preferred that this be done with an existing product.

A majority of the venture capitalists rejected price competition as a competitive strategy. Any advantages won through price competition were too easily lost, said one. The difficulties in achieving lower production costs than an established firm usually were too great for a modestly capitalized venture. Those who did not reject price competition considered it a less desirable approach to be taken only rarely.

Political strategies or commitments to alliance were seen as valuable, particularly by the high-tech specialists. A major customer's advance commitment, contingent only on performance, was useful, they agreed, but "you don't often see it," added one. Another venture capitalist remarked, "They (entrepreneurs) are not going to come to me if they've got this."

Although unanimous in considering strategy important, the interviewed venture capitalists were divided on the usefulness of the typical business plans submitted to them. One said they were "not that specific. All their strategies look rather similar." But the others relied more on the written plan. One even said, "If you can't write it down, we doubt that you can execute it."

Other Factors Considered Important

Several other factors emerged from the interviews that were not readily classified as entrepreneur or industry characteristics or as venture business strategy. These were not primary criteria to the venture capitalists who mentioned them but nevertheless were considered by them.

One such factor was the time until the venture would break even. One venture capitalist wanted new ventures to break even beginning in the second year following his investment; another was less precise but said he would no longer wait several years. Although not all venture types or strategies would be affected by reduced investor patience, this change appears to work against strategies based on building market share through price-cutting entry. If so, it reinforces the venture capitalists' expressed preference against price competition as a venture business strategy, and suggests a major difference between them and Biggadike's suggestions for corporate-sponsored new ventures.[22]

The preferences and opinions of the investors in his private firm influenced one venture capitalist. This influence was evident in his investment decision process, which included what he called "give and take" with them. Although none of the interviewed venture capitalists enjoyed absolute autonomy in his investment decisions, no one else shared so much of his authority with his investors. More common was an investment committee or similar arrangement involving other venture capitalists within the same organization. The difference reflected the different desires and abilities of the investors in the funds. It affected the decision process, but did not appear to affect the criteria used.

Another additional factor was "the deal itself," said two of the interviewed venture capitalists. An otherwise acceptable venture might not receive funds because of an entrepreneur's resistance to yielding enough equity interest or managerial sovereignty, for example, or because of tax considerations. The venture capitalist acting for the private firm was an interesting example of a deal maker. He stated that for all the analyses and investigation that went into his work, the part he loved was making the deals. His capital was partly his own and partly that of his investors, and decision making was primarily his responsibility. In many ways he resembled the deal-jelling independent entrepreneur of Collins and Moore, the economic actor who combines resources independently of any risk-bearing role he may fill.[23] Still, even for him, the deal remained the means to the end.

Each of these additional factors was mentioned by only one or two of the interview participants, and then only as a lesser consideration. Taken together, they indicate that venture capitalists, much like strategists or managers in general, present infinite individual variations on basic themes. What needs to be appreciated and remembered, though, is the central importance and ubiquity of those basic themes.

Conclusions

The venture capitalists interviewed for this chapter do not depart significantly from the industry profile, except for being larger than average. In their criteria for evaluating new ventures they seem quite typical. These facts are important for two reasons. First, they support the literature-based portrayal of venture capitalists that was developed earlier in this chapter. The description of the weight accorded entrepreneurs' characteristics and venture business strategies in venture capitalists' criteria appears to be accurate or, at least, to reflect the stated practices of this sample. Second, the representativeness of the interviewed venture capitalists is important because two of them were sources of individual ventures used in my research.

The interviewed venture capitalists clearly did not deviate from their industry's conventional wisdom in placing the entrepreneur at the top of their list of factors to consider. The entrepreneur's dedication, energy, and cooperativeness were deemed crucial. Entrepreneurial experience weighed almost as heavily, and unsuccessful experience meant almost certain disqualification by two of the five interview subjects.

Despite the importance of their (and their venture capital network's) subjective appraisal of an entrepreneur, all the venture capitalists also had preferences regarding both industry and strategy. Fragmented, growing industries were preferred, but mature industries were acceptable to each venture capitalist provided some sort of differentiation were possible. The attractiveness of differentiation carried over to strategy considerations, too, as every one of the interview subjects looked for it in a venture's strategy. Positioning in a niche or segment was vastly preferred to price competition.

The criteria expressed in these interviews, in Tyebjee and Bruno's research,[24] and in the conventional wisdom of venture capitalists represent a practical recipe for success in evaluating the more ambitious types of new ventures. As such, they are a starting point for researchers who wish to develop a theory of new venture performance. Like most practitioner recipes, this one is not fully articulated and lacks clear definitions of many variables. The willingness of some venture capitalists to invest occasionally in defiance of their own prescriptions suggests that they are not absolutely confident of their recipe or that there are additional portions of it that amount to modifications of what has been articulated.

What emerges from the venture capital industry's wisdom is far from being a model of new venture performance and lacks the rigor of a theory or even a conceptual framework. Too much remains unspecified or unexamined. But the venture capitalists' track record at least justifies using the key factors in their criteria (entrepreneur, strategy, and industry) as an indication of where to turn for help in the academic literature. Chapter 3 will take up the search for useful theory and research on new venture performance, especially as it relates to these three factors.

Notes

1. Karl H. Vesper, *New Venture Strategies* (Englewood Cliffs, N.J.: Prentice-Hall, 1980), p. 48.

2. Louis L. Allen, *Starting and Succeeding in Your Own Small Business* (New York: Grosset & Dunlap, 1968), p. 22. Emphasis in the original.

3. Ibid.

4. Ibid.

5. Norman D. Fast, "Venture Capital Investment and Technology Development," in *Frontiers of Entrepreneurship Research,* edited by Karl H. Vesper. (Wellesley, Mass.: Babson College Center for Entrepreneurial Studies, 1982), p. 289.

6. As venture capitalists found the number of portfolio companies per venture capital manager doubling from 1982 to 1984, they responded by reducing their investments in startups. See Udayan Gupta, "Stretched to the Limit," *Venture* 7 (June 1985):38–44.

7. The background and conclusions concerning CDCs are detailed by Frederick J. Beste III, "Community Development Corporations and Economic Development Commissions," pp. 63–71, and Jeffry A. Timmons, "Venture Capital in Sweden," pp. 294–312, both in *Frontiers of Entrepreneurship Research,* edited by Karl H. Vesper (Wellesley, Mass.: Babson College Center For Entrepreneurial Studies, 1982. The critical comparison between CDCs and venture capitalists is pursued in William R. Sandberg, "The Determinants of New Venture Performance: Strategy, Industry Structure and Entrepreneur, Ph.D. diss. Athens, Ga.: The University of Georgia, 1984.

8. Fast, "Venture Capital Investment," p. 289.

9. James M. Johnson, "Determinants of Unsuccessful Risk Capital Funding by Small Business," *American Journal of Small Business* 4 (July 1979):31–38.

10. Vesper, *New Venture Strategies.*

11. John R. Dominguez, *Venture Capital* (Lexington, Mass.: D.C. Heath, 1974), p. 13.

12. Alexander L. M. Dingee, Jr., Leonard E. Smollen, and Brian Haslett, "Characteristics of a Successful Entrepreneur," in *How to Raise Venture Capital,* edited by Stanley E. Pratt (New York: Charles Scribner's Sons, 1982), pp. 15–26.

13. Arnold C. Cooper, "Strategic Management: New Ventures and Small Busi-

ness," in *Strategic Management,* edited by Dan E. Schendel and Charles W. Hofer (Boston: Little, Brown, 1979), p. 321.

14. Johnson, "Determinants of Unsuccessful Risk Capital Funding."
15. Dingee, Smollen, and Haslett, "Characteristics of a Successful Entrepreneur."
16. Allen, *Starting and Succeeding,* p. 35.
17. A. David Silver, *Characteristics of Successful Entrepreneurs* (New York: Comptere, 1978), p. 15.
18. Dominguez, *Venture Capital.*
19. Tyzoon T. Tyebjee and Albert V. Bruno, "A Model of Venture Capitalist Investment Activity," *Management Science* 30 (1984):1051–1066.
20. Jon Levine, "The Venture Capital 100: Once Again, It's a Buyer's Market," *Venture* 4 (June 1982):80–90.
21. Levine, "The Venture Capital 100"; Richard Loftin, "What Venture Capitalists Want," *Inc.* 3 (November 1981):144–147.
22. E. Ralph Biggadike, *Corporate Diversification: Entry, Strategy, and Performance* (Boston: Graduate School of Business, Harvard University, 1979).
23. Orvis F. Collins and David G. Moore, *The Enterprising Man* (East Lansing, Mich.: Michigan State University, 1964).
24. Tyebjee and Bruno, "Model of Venture Capitalist."

3
Entrepreneurship and New Venture Performance in Theory and Research

In this chapter I present, interpret, and integrate theory and research on entrepreneurship and new venture performance. The literature is diverse and has not been well integrated. In Chapter 3 I bring it together, sort it out, and examine it critically. The purpose of this chapter is to prepare the *academic framework* that will be used in chapter 4 to synthesize a new conceptual framework of new venture performance.

The chapter begins with a definition of the entrepreneur as conceived for this thesis. Next I lay out the three principal areas into which the theory and research will be organized: (1) characteristics of the entrepreneur; (2) the industry entered and its structure; and (3) the venture business strategy. Special attention is paid to the role of strategy in determining performance of established businesses, and a parallel effect on new ventures is suggested.

Most of this chapter consists of the review of the three primary topics listed above. There follows a review of literature on aspects of the following topics that are related to new ventures and entrepreneurship: business failure and its prediction, the performance of both corporate-launched and independent new ventures, the stages of industry evolution and the product life cycle, and the strategies of low market share businesses.

The chapter concludes with a comparison of the states of theory and research in the subject areas reviewed here.

The Entrepreneur Defined

The definition of "the entrepreneur" and the conception of the entrepreneurial role in a social, economic, or corporate context have remained slippery and elusive. Economists have not reached a consensus on these points and thus have not provided a common understanding on which other fields can draw. This may partially explain the similar absence of consensus in the management literature. The following two sections compare economists' and management writers' approaches to defining the entrepeneur and conceiving of the entrepreneurial role.

Economists' Approaches to the Entrepreneur

The entrepreneur's role has been analyzed by many economists over the past century and more. Even so, "there is perhaps no other area of economic analysis where there exists less agreement."[1] The entrepreneur's personality has not received so much attention, for "economics, in speaking of entrepreneurs, has in view not men, but a definite function."[2] Major interpretations of the entrepreneurial role have conceived its function as bearing risk, managing uncertainty, innovating, and exploiting disequilibrium. Each of these roles will be discussed in turn.

Adam Smith saw the entrepreneur as a risk bearer, a source of capital. His contemporaries in France, notably Cantillon and Jean Baptiste Say, saw this role but also discerned a second, distinct entrepreneurial role that comprised owning, planning, organizing, and supervising, but not the bearing of risk.[3]

Frank Knight developed the concept of the entrepreneur as a manager of uncertainty. If perfect knowledge prevailed, as in models of perfect competition, uncertainty would not exist. Because of the "inexactness of the organizations and the imperfections of markets,"[4] however, "the primary problem or function is deciding what to do and how to do it."[5] The entrepreneur earns profits by bearing this responsibility created by economic change. Although change may result from conscious innovation, it affects both the innovators and other enterprises in diverse, sometimes unanticipated ways because it embodies errors in decisions made both in causing and in adapting to change.[6]

The concept of the entrepreneur-as-innovator owes its popularity to Joseph Schumpeter. His analysis begins with a general equilibrium, in which all markets are perfectly competitive and consumer tastes and producer technologies are given. The entrepreneur upsets this equilibrium by carrying out "new combinations of the means of production and credit."[7] For a time this act brings pure profits, but imitators eventually erase these profits and drive the economy back to equilibrium. Over time, economic progress is brought through a series of such lurches from one static equilibrium to another.

Schumpeter described the entrepreneur as being motivated by "the joy of creating, of getting things done, or simply of exercising one's energy and ingenuity." This person gladly confronts difficulties, enjoys change for change's sake, and "delights in ventures."[8] The entrepreneur may serve in any of a wide range of organizational positions, and may be with the firm for but a short time, so long as he directs some new combination of the means of production and credit. On the issue of risk bearing, Schumpeter was clear: "The entrepreneur is never the risk bearer."[9] Whatever financial commitment he makes is made as a capitalist, not as an entrepreneur.

Our discussion thus far has focused on the conceptual origins of the entrepreneurial role. The entrepreneur increasingly was seen not as a bearer of risk but as a manager of uncertainty and an innovator, who devises and implements new ways of doing business (Schumpeter's "new combinations of the means of production and credit"). Market imperfections or disequilibrium are seen either as giving rise to the entrepreneurial role (as in Knight's view) or being created by entrepreneurial innovation (as in Schumpeter's view).

Curiously, perhaps, modern specialists in the economics of the firm have neglected the entrepreneurial role. The firm is studied in microeconomics, and specifically in price theory, but is viewed as a rational calculator of input and output prices that accordingly produces a profit-maximizing quantity. The firm operates within an equilibrium state in which all participants have perfect knowledge of factor prices, demand, production functions, and technology. In short, there is neither a role for the innovator nor room for the assumption of uncertainty. As Kirzner put it, "It is well known that in price theory the entrepreneur has no place in the state of equilibrium."[10]

It might seem that Schumpeter's entrepreneur-as-innovator would satisfy Kirzner's criticism of price theory. After all, Schumpeter's entrepreneur is far more than a reflexive administrator who calculates optimal production quantities from known price and cost data. But Kirzner approached the entrepreneur from the perspective of the Austrian school of economics. Austrians conceive of entrepreneurial activity as comprising several functions: obtaining economic information, economic calculation, the "act of will" by which goods are assigned to the production process, and supervision of the production plan's execution.[11]

Austrian economics is subjectivist. It emphasizes the vital role of a person's awareness of relevant circumstances as well as the role of the circumstances themselves. This subjectivist perspective underlies the Austrian emphasis on obtaining information and leads to a parallel emphasis on the effects of ignorance and error. In the absence of complete and accurate information, buyers and sellers rationally agree on "uneconomic" prices that differ from those that would prevail under conditions of perfect knowledge.[12] The Austrians argue that economists who maintain the assumption of perfect knowledge cannot adequately treat many economic phenomena, including entrepreneurship.

The vital combination of knowledge, ignorance, and error leads to entrepreneurial action. The entrepreneur acts not on the basis of past and present conditions but on a vision of the future. As Austrian economist Ludwig von Mises put it, the successful entrepreneur "sees the past and the present as other people do; but he judges the future in a different way."[13] The unsuccessful entrepreneur likewise sees potential profit in a different vision of the future. Because market participants have differing information and perceptions, "uneconomic" prices prevail; at this stage the difference between the successful and the unsuccessful entrepreneur is in the ultimate accuracy of their expectations. Right or wrong, though, "the real entrepreneur is a speculator, . . . eager to utilize his opinions about the future structure of the market."[14]

The key insight garnered from the Austrian school's theories of entrepreneurship is that the entrepreneur is *not* upsetting an equilibrium state, even when upsetting the status quo. Instead the economy moves toward equilibrium to the extent that the entrepreneur correctly anticipates future conditions and facilitates other individuals' efforts to achieve their own objectives. Disequilibrium is a necessary condition for entrepreneurial success, not a consequence of it.

Disequilibrium also plays a key part in Edith Penrose's theory of the growth of the firm.[15] She referred to "interstices" in a growing economy—opportunities for growth that existing large firms, regardless of their competitive advantages, are not in a position to exploit because they prefer to devote their limited resources to greater opportunities elsewhere. Penrose noted that if small firms cannot exploit them, there will be opportunities for new firms either in entirely new industries or in industries that grow more rapidly than the capacity of their existing firms.

In sum, economists have conceived of the entrepreneur in terms of the various entrepreneurial activities or functions. Dealing with the uncertain future is a common element in their analyses, whether the economist is Knight, Schumpeter, or one of the modern Austrians. Whether the entrepreneur is seen as the ultimate bearer of uncertainty or risk, or as its creator, the theme of risk is present. The Austrians add the precondition of disequilibrium and the effects of ignorance, error and differences in knowledge, which animate entrepreneurial competition.

The Entrepreneur in the Management Literature

Management literature has conceived of the entrepreneur in a number of ways. While venture initiation is a characteristic that unites most of these views of the entrepreneur, they differ on the entrepreneur's risk bearing, risk creation, source of compensation, and long-term organizational affiliation.

Frederick Webster reviewed this literature and usefully identified five entrepreneurial archetypes found therein.[16] Two of them, the small business owner/operator and the administrative entrepreneur, characterize the prevalent concepts. These two types have much in common: They are risk takers but not risk creators, they found a firm and remain affiliated with it over an extended period, and they are compensated through both salary and profits. In fact, they differ in only one respect: The owner/operator does not seek capital gains because he retains ownership of the firm. A third type, the independent entrepreneur, is much rarer in the management literature. This entrepreneur *does* create risk but does not bear it, operates in a venture framework without a long-term affiliation with a firm, and is compensated entirely through capital gains.

Several distinctions should be noted within these types. Liles recognized three categories of surviving new ventures, the most common being the "marginal firms" whose owners accept low incomes (frequently less than they could have earned elsewhere) in order to be self-employed. Two less common types are more successful. The "high-potential venture" is intended to grow rapidly and become a large corporation. The "attractive small company" "is not intended to become a large corporation, probably will never have a public market for its stock, and will not be attractive to most venture capital investors."[17] Susbauer has pointed out that while some companies are "conscious underachievers" that sacrifice growth for owners' values, what seems to be an "attractive small company" may actually be an "unconscious underachiever" falling short of its potential because of mismatched technology, market, finance, or management capabilities.[18]

The distinctions based on intentions and on conscious versus unconscious underachievement are fundamental to sorting out types of new ventures. They are at the heart of the distinction between entrepreneurs and entrepreneurial ventures, on the one hand, and small business owners and small business ventures on the other. Profit-oriented and growth-oriented goals, innovative behavior, and strategic management practices have been associated with entrepreneurs and their ventures.[19]

The management literature clearly has not fallen into the economists' habit of viewing entrepreneurs as performers of functions rather than as people. On the other hand, this literature has given little explicit attention to the entrepreneur's economic role. The role referred to here is not merely that which is comprehended in studies of the number of jobs (or percentage of the GNP, or so on) attributable to new or small businesses. Instead, it is the equilibrium-making or equilibrium-breaking role described by economists.

What emerges from the management literature's view of the entrepreneur is a portrait that complements the economists' conception. We see something more of the tradeoffs among values that animate the somewhat austere, functional portrayal favored by many economists: This entrepreneur may prefer independence to income and therefore remain an independent business owner even when returns could be increased through other employment or the transformation of the business into a larger, professionally managed organization. But unless we embrace the Austrian economists' contributions as well, we lose the insights that the management literature has only recently begun to state formally—the importance of disequilibrium and of subjective evaluation in the entrepreneur's role and decisions.

The Entrepreneur as Conceived in This Book

The entrepreneur as conceived in this book might best be described as someone who undertakes to initiate and aggrandize a profit-oriented business unit, with financial returns the measure of success. The new business unit is expected to operate over a period that allows an appreciable measure of freedom of decision and during which the entrepreneur hopes to exploit a perceived market opportunity.

This entrepreneur represents only a subset of entrepreneurs as conceived by others. The definition includes only startup entrepreneurs, the only type included in my research sample. In reviewing the literature, however, this book will use "entrepreneur" in its broader sense, and will specify "startup entrepreneur" when a distinction seems in order. In particular, a distinction will be maintained between *entrepreneurial* experience and *startup* experience, which is a special instance of entrepreneurial experience.

This book's conception of the entrepreneur also excludes a large proportion of those who establish new businesses. The founder of an intendedly marginal firm is not covered by this definition. The design of this research has substantially reduced the likelihood of any intendedly marginal firms being studied because few of those would approach a venture capitalist. If a firm in my research sample eventually came to resemble a marginal firm, it is likely that the metamorphosis was unintended, at least at the venture's inception.[20]

In sum, not all so-called entrepreneurs could appear in this book, but all of the venture founders captured in this book can be considered entrepreneurs. With this conception established, we turn to a review of the academic literature on entrepreneurs.

Theory and Research on Entrepreneurship and New Venture Performance

A vast range of studies offer a wealth of information about entrepreneurs and entrepreneurship. Their focus may be as broad as a nation's social system or as narrow as the traits of one selected entrepreneur; their purpose may be related only tangentially to the study of entrepreneurs' characteristics or new venture performance.[21] In a major review of new venture literature, Arnold Cooper noted the scarcity of research on the relationships among characteristics of entrepreneurs, venture strategy, and venture performance.[22] The need was especially great for research on the strategy–performance relationship.

Cooper suggested that important dimensions of this relationship might include the product–market choice, the business strategy, and the industry's stage of evolution.

A researcher's challenge, then, is to organize the available information in a way that yields insights into the relationships between new venture performance and other variables of interest. Cooper has provided one way to view the new venture literature, by focusing on three stages in the life of a growing firm: the startup stage, early growth, and later growth. Within the startup stage, he distinguished between the decision to found a venture and other decisions concerning competitive strategy. These early strategic decisions, he suggested, help shape the firm's future development.

In considering first the decision to start a business, Cooper viewed the research question as one of understanding why and whether persons with certain characteristics become entrepreneurs. Then he broadened his focus to include the performance of the venture, and specifically the effects of strategy on that performance.

My review of the literature is organized to highlight the topics that seem germane to new venture performance. I concentrate on the relationship between each topic and new venture performance. Thus the areas of primary interest are the theory and research relating new venture performance to (1) the characteristics of the entrepreneur; (2) the type of industry entered; and (3) the venture business strategy. Because the mere propensity for entrepreneurship is not of central importance in this book, much of the research on entrepreneurs is not particularly relevant to our purpose and will not be discussed.

Ideally, the research issues raised in this book should be addressed from a multidimensional perspective, since they ask how the entrepreneur, industry, and strategy combine to affect venture performance. A review of the new venture literature found only a few examples of multiple-factor theory or research. Most prior research has emphasized one or another of these factors to the exclusion of the others. Therefore it was necessary to review and integrate essentially separate literatures from the several areas of interest.

The following sections present performance-related information from the literature on the characteristics of entrepreneurs, on the type of industry, and on the venture business strategy. Subsequent sections will draw on the literature in related areas, including business failure, the performance of ventures, industry evolution, and strategies for low market share businesses.

Characteristics of the Entrepreneur

The characteristics of the entrepreneur that interest new venture researchers fall under two broad headings: the entrepreneur's experience and the entrepreneur's psychology.

Table 3–1
Descriptions of Principal Studies Relating Entrepreneur's Characteristics to Venture Performance

Study	*Sample*	*Years' Data*	*Factors Examined*
Hoad and Rosko (1964)	95 Michigan manufacturers founded in 1960	3	Management practices Owner/manager of a similar business Owner/manager of any business Nonmanagerial experience in a similar business Managerial experience in consumer versus industrial businesses
Collins and Moore (1964)	150 managers in 110 manufacturers founded between 1945 and 1958, surviving 1962; 40 given TAT	4–17	Activity within firm Family background Administrative structure Plans for firm's future
Smith (1967)	52 of subjects from Collins and Moore (1964)	At least 5	Craftsman vs. Opportunistic entrepreneurs Rigid vs. Adaptable firms
Cooper (1971)	30 founders of 1960s high-tech startups in California	Various	Impetus to start the venture Motivation Role of incubator organizations Prior entrepreneurial experience

The Entrepreneur's Experience

According to Buchele, one of "the three main mistakes made in starting new firms" is that "the key persons do not have rounded managerial experience in the particular line of business."[23] Nearly all the discursive writers and much of the research on new ventures and entrepreneurs deem "experience" important. Exactly what is meant by the word varies, though. Broadly interpreted, it comprises experience as a manager, in major functional disciplines, in a particular line of business, and as a startup entrepreneur, as well as education or training. Most researchers have focused on more than one aspect of experience, but few have covered all of them.

Studies by Hoad and Rosko, Collins and Moore, Smith, and Cooper offer the most useful base of information on entrepreneurs' experience as it relates to performance. They deal specifically with new ventures and their founders or with entrepreneurs who had founded companies, and three of them measure venture performance. The coverage of these studies is summarized in table 3–1.

Of the four studies, Hoad and Rosko[24] probably came closest to explaining new venture performance, for their sample included successful, marginal, and failed firms. Although they reported frequency data, Hoad and Rosko performed no statistical tests. As will be noted below, some of their reported findings did not attain acceptable levels of statistical significance.

Collins and Moore [25] used a sample of firms that were at least four years old by the end of their data collection phase. Thus their entrepreneurs could be considered fairly successful, at least by the standard of avoiding failure during venture initiation. Collins and Moore interviewed these entrepreneurs *after* their startups, however, so may have observed the effects rather than the causes of success. They did attempt to provide a control group for comparison purposes, but chose the male population of Michigan, controlled for age. This did not permit a contrast between successful and failed entrepreneurs.

Smith[26] had conducted many of the interviews for Collins and Moore, and used about one-third of their sample for his own study. Creating ideal types, he found near-perfect pairings of Craftsman-Entrepreneurs with Rigid companies and of Opportunistic-Entrepreneurs with Adaptable companies. The latter group showed far greater sales growth, and Smith argued that this type of entrepreneur had the characteristics required for adaptation. While Smith's position was tenable, it could not be proved because of the absence of Craftsman-Adaptable pairs in his sample.

Cooper[27] studied a different type of venture and, presumably, entrepreneur. He acknowledged the possible differences between his sample and entrepreneurs in general and the probable underrepresentation of failed ventures in his sample of high-tech California startups. While venture performance was not a primary interest of Cooper's study, it was measured.

The following sections draw on these and other studies for evidence on the impact of the entrepreneur's characteristics on new venture performance.

Managerial Experience. The value of undifferentiated managerial experience is dubious, according to most observers. Buchele stated that an entrepreneur's management skills are not transferable from one line of business to another because small firms cannot afford the staff specialists necessary to help a generalist learn the unique aspects of his new business.[28] Others deprecated the value of experience in unrelated businesses, while stressing the importance of experience in the same line of business.

Supporters of the value of undifferentiated managerial experience have been unable to furnish convincing evidence. Smith reported greater success among entrepreneurs who had managerial skills and orientation rather than those of an artisan.[29] Once again, though, the composition of his sample prevented proof of his position. Hoad and Rosko argued that management experience, even in an unrelated business, is important.[30] However, their own data failed to indicate any relationship between venture performance and years of experience as a business owner–manager.[31]

Functional Area Experience. Buchele stated the consensus view when he explained that the necessary "rounded managerial experience" implied enough experience in selling, design, production, accounting, and finance "to appreciate the subspecialties in each."[32] Support for this view has been anecdotal for the most part, although Hoad and Rosko showed that good performance was associated with good accounting records and seeking the advice of outside accountants.[33] In studies of technology-based new ventures, multifunction management backgrounds have been reported as characteristics of successful ventures [34] and as a factor that distinguishes higher from lower performers.[35]

Experience in the Line of Business. The anecdotal evidence and arguments in the discursive literature are clear: "Perhaps the most inexcusable mistake of all is that of a person starting a business in which he has had no experience."[36] Hoad and Rosko reported that venture success was positively related to experience as an owner or manager in a similar business. The performance differences in their data have been found not to be significant, although the observed differences are in the reported direction.[37]

An interesting pattern appears in Hoad and Rosko's data. The proportion of both successes and failures increase with increased experience, while marginal firms are much less frequent. Two explanations seem plausible. First, a highly experienced entrepreneur may be more likely to gamble heavily on a potential breakthrough in product design or market segmentation. Someone with less experience in the business may be less likely to devise such a bold stroke, whether good or bad. Thus the experienced entrepreneur is more likely to win big or to lose big.

A second possibility is that the more experienced entrepreneurs include relatively more of the veteran craftsmen. Smith reported that craftsmen's inflexibility impaired the growth of their firms.[38] Such inflexibility could also be expected to jeopardize the early survival and growth of a new venture.

Startup Experience. Many researchers have concluded that a prior startup provides invaluable experience. Collins and Moore portrayed the entrepreneur as spending several years trying to establish a business, all the while learning how to "jell" deals. The entrepreneur learns, sometimes at great personal cost, "the basic technique of entrepreneurship: the bringing together of ideas, people, and money in a profitable arrangement."[33] Along the way, one or more attempts are likely to fail, yet the entrepreneur may profit from the experience.

Lamont confirmed the value of startup experience in his study of 24 technology-based new ventures.[40] Those whose entrepreneurs had prior startup experience showed superior sales growth, profitability, and financial strength. These firms had a clearer product–market orientation and had hired more management talent in key functional areas than the other new ventures. Lamont believed the experienced entrepreneurs had learned the importance of these factors and that this learning from experience implied that would-be entrepreneurs could learn from the experiences of successful entrepreneurs. It seems reasonable, then, to consider formal education as an alternative to experience.

Education and Training. Efforts to establish the value of education for entrepreneurs have yielded mixed but generally positive results. In technical fields it is often a virtual prerequisite. Even in nontechnical areas, education appears to help. Whereas some early studies questioned the importance of a college education, more recent data show entrepreneurs to be more highly educated than the general adult population[41] but less so than corporate executives.[42]

Whether education improves performance is less certain than how much education entrepreneurs have been getting,[43] but most research has shown a positive relationship. A "failure syndrome" found among 359 financially troubled SBA clients included both an absence and a derision of formal education.[44] Hoad and Rosko found that "education makes a difference when it extends a year or more beyond high school."[45] They found higher rates of both success and failure among educated entrepreneurs and a higher rate of marginal ventures among uneducated entrepreneurs.

Hoad and Rosko cross-tabulated education and managerial experience in a similar line of business. The educated–experienced entrepreneur performed best, but the least likely to fail was the uneducated–inexperienced entrepreneur. The latter type's success rate was lower than any other, but a high proportion of these ventures were marginal. Hoad and Rosko concluded that these were probably skilled craftsmen seeking wage-substitute returns as entrepreneurs rather than hire out as employees.[46]

The value of education crystallizes among high-tech entrepreneurs. Cooper's 30 successful entrepreneurs included 29 college graduates, 14 of whom had graduate degrees.[47] In an interesting twist, Roberts found that high-performing entrepreneurs typically had master's degrees, whereas lower performers typically had doctorates.[48] He commented that the temperament, attitude, and orientation of the Ph.D. usually are inconsistent with the demands of entrepreneurship.

The Entrepreneur's Psychology

The entrepreneur's psychology and personality have been studied mainly to determine what leads a person to entrepreneurship. Less attention has been devoted to their effects on success or failure as an entrepreneur. The following review will include both types of study, but will give greater emphasis to entrepreneurial performance. The subtopics considered here reflect the areas researched most thoroughly: the entrepreneur's need for achievement, beliefs as to locus of control, and risk preferences.

Need for Achievement. A good working definition of need for achievement (*n* Ach) is "a need to excel in relation to competitive or internalized standards."[49] The concept owes its widespread recognition largely to the work of McClelland, who associated it with desires for personal responsibility for solving problems, moderate goals and risks, and concrete feedback on performance.[50]

The link between *n* Ach and entrepreneurship remains controversial. McClelland[51] found a clear relationship between high *n* Ach and the subsequent holding of "entrepreneurial" positions among male college alumni, but defined "entrepreneurial" far more broadly than in most research. Using a narrower definition, subsequent research has attempted to relate *n* Ach to entrepreneurial performance. Successful entrepreneurs were found to score higher than the general population on *n* Ach or similar achievement value measures.[52] Efforts to inculcate or stimulate *n* Ach in current or would-be entrepreneurs have brought unclear results. They have been declared successful,[53] of limited value in the absence of business skills or training, [54] and of questionable effectiveness.[55]

Researchers have reached conflicting conclusions in the case of the high-technology entrepreneur, too. Schrage found that high *n* Ach was associated with both high profits and large losses, whereas low *n* Ach was associated with more moderate results.[56] He explained that the high *n* Ach entrepreneur strives harder to succeed, but this exceptional striving only worsens performance if the entrepreneur is misguided or receives poor feedback. Wainer and Rubin attributed Schrage's findings to poor scoring of research protocols; their own sample showed high *n* Ach associated with rapid company growth but no performance difference between medium and low *n* Ach entrepreneurs.[57]

One impediment to the use of *n* Ach to understand or predict entrepreneurial behavior and performance has been the need for psychologists to administer and score projective tests. Researchers have made only modest progress in developing or discovering standard tests to do the job more easily and more effectively. A more general impediment has been the inability of researchers to discover a link between *n* Ach and key aspects of entrepreneurial performance.[58]

Locus of Control Beliefs. Locus of control describes an individual's beliefs about his own ability to determine the outcomes of events in his life. A person with *external* beliefs thinks that luck, chance, fate, or other people are in control of the outcomes or that events are simply unpredictable. Belief that one's own behavior or characteristics determine outcomes is considered a belief in *internal* control.[59]

Internal-control beliefs affect the decision to start a venture because that decision depends on an entrepreneur's belief that he will be able to control the venture's outcome.[60] Researchers have found significantly more internal scores among students planning to start businesses than those who did not plan to do so[61] and more among entrepreneurs than in nearly all population groups previously measured.[62] But entrepreneurs and corporate managers did not differ significantly, and both were more internal than most groups.[63]

Brockhaus compared scores obtained in 1975 from owners of businesses that were less than three months old. Those whose businesses survived in 1978 had significantly more internal beliefs than the others. He concluded that the external entrepreneurs may have been resigned to accepting rather than reversing unfavorable outcomes to such a degree that they were more likely to slide into failure.[64]

Before accepting Brockhaus's conclusion as directly applicable to the type of new venture to be studied in this book, a major qualification should be considered. His sample was drawn from the list of business licenses obtained in St. Louis County, Missouri, during a two-month period. Although Brockhaus did not describe the types of businesses involved, it seems safe to assume that a goodly proportion were the classic "mom 'n pop" stores that predominate among business startups but that are not the type of venture of interest in this book.

There is another limitation to the value of locus of control in this book. It is probable that very few external entrepreneurs would even bother to approach venture capitalists or investment bankers—indeed, the very act of preparing a business plan would seem at best folly, and at worst an act of hubris, to a decidedly external person. Irrespective of the statistical validity of Brockhaus's research, it is likely to be of little use to someone screening more ambitious venture proposals.

Risk Preferences. The concept of risk used in entrepreneurship research has become richly variegated. In addition to traditional financial risk, the concept has broadened to include opportunity costs and psychic costs of venturing and of failing.[65] With risk defined as the probability of failure, entrepreneurs have been said to prefer moderate levels of risk and to be less risk averse than managers.[66]

Brockhaus has challenged the general belief that moderate risk preferences distinguish entrepreneurs.[67] Comparing his earlier sample of startup entrepreneurs to corporate managers who had changed companies and those who had changed positions within a company, Brockhaus found no significant differences in risk preferences. Nor were the entrepreneurs significantly different from the general population.

Brockhaus also compared successful and failed entrepreneurs on the basis of risk preference measurements taken when they received their business licenses.[68] No difference was found between the two groups. Brockhaus tentatively has concluded that risk preference "may not be related to either the entrepreneurial decision, or to the success of the enterprise."[69]

Summary of Entrepreneur's Characteristics and Performance

The entrepreneur's managerial experience was found to be of little value unless it was in a business similar to the new venture. Functional-area experience was said to be valuable in general and in high-technology ventures. Hoad and Rosko[70] remain the principal source of data on the effects of these varieties of experience on venture performance.

Startup experience was found to be important in each of the studies that examined it. The evidence is not so quantitative, but those who offer nonquantified judgments are firm in their belief.[71] Education appears to be of great importance only to high-technology entrepreneurs.

Research on the entrepreneur's psychology has been primarily descriptive and has not established causal relationships between personal characteristics and new venture performance. A high *n* Ach, which characterizes successful entrepreneurs, may just as strongly characterize unsuccessful ones; measurements taken after either outcome may tell little about the entrepreneur's characteristics prior to the attempt. Nor has risk preference proved a distinguishing characteristic of entrepreneurs or of successful entrepreneurs.

Some distinction can be made between likely successful and likely unsuccessful entrepreneurs on the basis of their locus of control beliefs, but it seems safe to assume that those who take the initiative to approach venture capitalists have internal locus of control beliefs. Therefore the distinction is likely to be lost in the present research sample.

Characteristics of the Industry

It will be recalled that there are three areas of primary interest in developing the foundation for this book. One—the characteristics of the entrepreneur—has been found to lack established causal relationships with venture performance. The two that remain—industry characteristics and venture strategy—

are thought to play important roles in shaping a firm's development. We now take up the performance effects of the industry chosen for a new venture.

In comparison to the characteristics of the entrepreneur, there has been little research on the effect of an industry on new venture performance. Even so, there is enough evidence to lead Vesper to call the entrepreneur's choice of product or service "probably the most important variable affecting the survival and success of a new venture."[72]

Management and entrepreneurship writers traditionally approached this important topic by classifying industries according to the economic function performed or the nature of the industry's inputs or outputs. Thus industries have been described as retail or wholesale, manufacturing or service, and so on, with high-technology industries receiving special treatment.

Such classifications predominate in the research described in the preceding portions of this chapter. For example, Hoad and Rosko classified their 95 firms into 4 groups: industrial process, industrial end product, consumer durable, and consumer nondurable. They classified performance as successful, marginal, or failed but performed no statistical tests.[73]

Vesper compared the new venture survival rates reported by studies of various industries. He concluded that "survival rates for new ventures tend to vary with industry," which he attributed to some fields being more promising, whereas others were crowded and highly competitive.[74]

Although the studies cited by Vesper have similarities in their definitions of survival and in the years they covered, there are enough differences to weaken and limit comparisons. The studies differed in such key respects as the regions represented, the age of the firms studied, the year of data collection, and the specificity of their industry classifications. Thus comparisons across studies may be highly unreliable. Moreover, neither Vesper nor Hoad and Rosko explained interindustry differences in generalizable terms.

Thus the question remains unanswered: What factors distinguish a "promising" field? The contrasts between "the promising field" and "one already crowded" and between failure "in the highly competitive business" and success in "the growing one" imply that there are significant differences other than the line of business. If crowded, competitive fields are unpromising irrespective of their line of business, then it may be that the characteristics that make them so are their crowdedness or their competitiveness—or some other characteristics. The traditional entrepreneurship literature does not explicitly consider this possibility and therefore is not helpful in identifying the factors that make a field or industry attractive for entry by a new venture.

Industrial organization (IO) economists have used a different approach to describing industries. They focus on the relationships through which the basic conditions of supply and demand and the market structure of an industry influence the performance of that industry and the conduct of the firms within it. Market structure refers to such industrywide parameters as the number of buyers and sellers, barriers to entry, product differentiation, cost structures, and the degree of vertical integration. Conduct refers to pricing and product strategy decisions, advertising, research and innovation activities, and other actions of the industry's member firms. IO also considers how firm conduct affects basic conditions and market structures.[75]

It remained for the IO paradigm and language to be adapted to the strategic plans and actions of individual firms and their managers.[76] Michael Porter has figured prominently in this adaptation and in its popularization. In examining the strategic decision to enter a new business, Porter wrote from the perspective of an existing firm.[77] Although this is not precisely the problem facing a startup entrepreneur, the entry plan entails consideration of the same structural factors in either case. The impact or seriousness of some factors may differ for new ventures, of course—one thinks of the consequences of their more limited management depth and staff support and of their possibly weaker position in capital markets—but the paradigm itself should remain valid.

Porter focused on two sources of deterrents to entry: structural barriers and the expected reactions of incumbent firms. Structural barriers may elevate the costs of entering an industry or may require extraordinary costs in order to compete effectively after entry. He identified six major market-based sources of barriers to entry:[78]

1. Economies of scale
2. Product differentiation
3. Capital requirements
4. Switching costs
5. Access to distribution channels
6. Cost disadvantages independent of scale

In addition, Porter noted that government policy is another major source of barriers to entry. Entry may be impeded or prevented by licensing, franchising, regulations and costs related to pollution and safety requirements, and other policies.

The second source of deterrents to entry—expected incumbent retaliation—is affected by both economic and noneconomic considerations. Retaliation may take the form of price cutting, increased promotional efforts, liberalized warranty or credit terms, product quality improvements, or expansion of capacity. Porter argued that retaliation is more likely (and entry more risky and therefore less attractive) in industries where the following conditions obtain:

1. Slow growth
2. Homogeneous products
3. High fixed costs
4. High concentration
5. Incumbents attach high strategic importance to their position
6. Incumbents' managements are disposed to retaliate because of their own attitudes

Porter also argued that retaliation is less likely if an industry lacks these conditions or if it possesses other characteristics, including the following:

1. High cost of retaliation relative to benefits
2. A paternal dominant firm or group that values order
3. Incumbents' abilities to retaliate are restricted by their need to protect current business
4. Incumbents adhere to conventional wisdom that locks them into less effective methods of competition

Because the combined effects of entry barriers and incumbents' retaliation can be enormous, Porter suggested, entry is attractive only if an industry is in such disequilibrium that above-normal profits will remain even after such effects are endured. An industry at equilibrium offers only normal profits; under ordinary circumstances, the average entrant will not be compensated for the higher risk associated with trying to overcome entry barriers. Disequilibrium frequently is associated with certain types of industries, he added. These include new industries (although the industry may be unattractive if development costs are high for the pioneer or if subsequent entries will not be more costly or difficult than the initial entry); those in which barriers to entry are likely to increase with time; and those that somehow remain obscure, escaping the attention and participation of many potential entrants.

In its emphasis on the importance of disequilibrium, Porter's analysis is consistent with the Austrian economists' conception of the entrepreneur. As was discussed earlier in this chapter, the Austrians see the entrepreneur as one who identifies and exploits disequilibrium. This contrasts sharply with the more popular conception, based on Schumpeter,[79] of the entrepreneur as the shatterer of equilibrium. If equilibrium is understood to mean merely the status quo, whatever its characteristics, then the popular conception is accurate. But if equilibrium is to be understood as economists intend (that is, a state of affairs in which perfect knowledge prevails and enables each participant to calculate correctly his optimum position within constraints imposed by correctly anticipated responses of others), there is no place for the alertness and boldness often attributed to the entrepreneur.[80]

Strategic management researchers were slow to incorporate market structure and other IO concepts in their work. A number of explanations have been offered for this slowness.[81] The most convincing explanations center on the fundamental differences between the IO and strategy fields: IO studied industries from a public policy viewpoint, unrealistically assumed that firms and managers were essentially homogeneous and devoid of emotions or objectives other than profit maximization, and used a static, cross-sectional paradigm that clung to determinism in exploring the relationship between market structure and firm conduct. In each respect, IO contradicted equally crucial assumptions and perspectives of the strategy field.

Porter has made the case for IO's potential contributions to strategic management, and thus to the understanding of firm performance, and has reviewed early progress toward the integration of these two fields.[82] Subsequent research has quickened the pace of integration and has enhanced our understanding of firm strategies and performance under various industry structural conditions.[83]

If strategic management researchers had applied IO concepts to the situations or challenges facing new ventures, there might be a clearer understanding of what factors influence new venture performance. No such general inquiry has been made, however.

As an alternative, one can refer to research on a topic that is vital to new ventures, such as industry entry. To date in the strategic management field, though, only Yip appears to have applied IO theory to industry entry.[84] Using Profit Impact of Marketing Strategy (PIMS) data and supplementary data from his PIMS sample,[85] he studied the effects of barriers to entry on the occurrence of entry, the prevalence of direct entry versus entry by acquisition, and entrant performance. In doing so, Yip operationalized Porter's theoretical model[86] and examined 69 entrants in 31 markets. He found market share gain, his measure of success, to be positively associated with the exit of competitors, with entrants having diversified parents, and with entrants having higher prices than incumbents. Having higher costs than incumbents and the size of an entrant's parent company were negatively associated with market share gain.

Two limitations must be recognized in attempting to apply Yip's findings to new ventures. First, he did not obtain entrant performance data other than market share; no financial performance data were available because Yip surveyed industry incumbents rather than the entrants themselves. Second, only 8 of 69 ventures in his sample were independent startups; the other 61 had corporate parents or were corporate acquisitions of incumbent firms. Hence the generalizability of Yip's findings to independent new ventures must remain in doubt.

The treatment of market structure by new venture researchers (or of independent ventures by researchers who have adopted the IO paradigm) is especially rare. What little there is tends not to be empirical but has begun to discuss industry or market structure. For example, Porter's descriptions of entry strategies and of embryonic industries have been applied to the early evolution of the U.S. automobile industry.[87] The major theoretical effort in this area has been made by Karl Vesper,[88] who associated higher returns to incumbents with difficult entry, high capital requirements, patents or similar protection for incumbents, strong customer ties to incumbents, and established reputations—essentially the structural barriers to entry identified by Porter.[89]

In order to extend IO's contributions to new venture performance, it is necessary to overcome most, if not all, of the obstacles that Porter[90] cited as retarding its adoption in strategic management research. This book has or will have dealt with the two fields' differing frames of reference, units of analysis, and views of the decision maker (regardless of whether entrepreneur or manager); the static versus dynamic views of industry structure; and the narrowness of earlier IO theory.

There now is theoretical, empirical, and practitioner support for the significance of industry structure. The next step, in terms of the evolving model of IO analysis, is to consider the importance of firm conduct. As noted earlier, firm conduct refers to actions with respect to pricing, product strategy, advertising, research, and innovation. These are among the decisions encompassed by competitive strategy. The next step, then, leads into the strategic management literature to consider the importance of the new venture's business strategy.

The Venture Business Strategy

It has already been observed that a multidimensional perspective is required to investigate the factors affecting new venture performance. Earlier discussion has centered on theory and research relating performance to the characteristics of entrepreneurs and to industry structure, and has found that few studies examined more than a narrow set of factors. The dearth of theory and research is most apparent in the area of venture business strategy, which is considered only infrequently, rarely explicitly, and never in conjunction with the entrepreneur or industry structure. Such neglect is not consistent with the central role accorded strategy in the strategic management literature.

Strategy's Importance in the Strategic Management Literature

Forming and acting upon a vision of the future, the essence of the Austrian economists' concept of entrepreneurship, are also at the heart of the teleological model of strategic management. Strategic management is understood as a process that deals with formulating and implementing an organization's strategy and, more broadly, with its entrepreneurial work, renewal, and growth.[91] Although this view encompasses a vast domain, its elements share a goal orientation that permits their integration. In strategic management, strategy formulation yields proposed strategies believed to be effective in relating present and planned resources to environmental threats and opportunities in the pursuit of organizational goals. The proposed strategies are evaluated against the environment and goals and a choice is made, after which the chosen strategy's implementation is controlled and monitored. The comparison of results with intended results may trigger the process anew.

Strategies deal with two questions: "What business(es) shall we be in?" and "How should we compete in a given business?"[92] Precise meanings of the term "strategy" have differed from one author to another, but most definitions are compatible with Hofer and Schendel's concept of strategy.[93] They identify four components of strategy: scope, distinctive competences, competitive advantages, and synergy. *Scope* is the extent of the firm's interactions with its environment, commonly described by the product–market segments in which it competes. *Distinctive competences* are those functions at which the firm is exceptionally skilled as a result of the types, amounts, and deployment of its resources. *Competitive advantage* is the firm's edge over its rivals, resulting from the concatenation of scope and resource decisions. (Note that the value to the firm of a particular distinctive competence depends on its usefulness in the firm's product–market segments.) *Synergy* is the joint effect of the firm's scope, distinctive competences, and competitive advantages as they cut across markets and organizational units.

The choice of businesses in which to compete is referred to as the corporate strategy decision. Its importance to a new venture, which is nearly always a single-business firm, is limited to the interindustry differences commonly described by IO researchers.

Strategy's importance at the business level has been noted, too, and is more to the point here. Hofer[94] defined strategic challenges at this level and compared the relative effectiveness of various responses that changed the business unit's way(s) of competing. These responses consisted of changes in the unit's scope, distinctive competences, and competitive advantages.

Others have narrowed their focus to the effects of strategy in specific industries, life-cycle stages, competitive positions, or other situations.[95] They have found that successful firms differed from less successful ones in their choice of strategies and in their adherence to certain strategic prescriptions.

Hofer and Schendel stated that their concept of strategy applied to small or single-business firms as well as to medium and large diversified firms.[96] The hierarchical nature of strategy and of strategy formulation would be compressed in a simpler organization, they added. Abell has suggested thinking of the entire question of scope (or business definition) in terms of the degree to which the resources used by the organization in various activities were related to each other.[97] Decisions made anywhere from the corporate level to the sub-business level, could involve choices of customer groups, customer functions, and technologies. Only through a firm's choice of organizational structure do these strategic choices become separated in any hierarchical sense.

Abell's insights indicate how the general concept of strategy and the gist of the strategic management research can be applied to new ventures. In the new venture, the full array of strategic decisions are made at the business level or below. Both the choice of industry and the choice of methods of competition are part of the new venture's strategy, as Cooper suggested.[98] The applicability of the concept of strategy to all firms, regardless of size or complexity, and the apparent link between strategy and performance point to the potential value of research on new venture strategies.

Research on Venture Business Strategy

Having seen that strategy affects the performance of business organizations in general and that the general concept of strategy is consistent with the types of decisions required of entrepreneurs, we turn to the literature on venture business strategy.

The meaning of strategy in the new venture context does not differ greatly from its meaning in the strategic management literature. However, the new venture literature lacks a parallel to strategic management's empirical research on the strategy–performance relationship. New venture strategic theory remains at an earlier stage of development. Nevertheless, there are conceptual schemes by which to classify strategies and theoretical support for a strategy–performance relationship similar to that found in strategic management. We shall now review the most useful of these schemes.

Vesper has provided the most complete treatment of new venture strategies.[99] He identified "entry wedges" with which a new venture could break into an industry. Two of his four "main competitive entry wedges," acquiring a going concern and acquiring a franchise, do not apply to the type of new venture covered in this book. The other two main wedges are a new product or service and parallel competition. These main wedges are opposites: Parallel competition relies on imitation or minor variations on an existing product or service.

Eleven "other entry wedges" fill supporting roles in Vesper's classification scheme. They come under 5 headings: exploiting partial momentum, customer sponsorship, parent company sponsorship, governmental sponsorship, and wedge combinations. (The 5 headings and 11 "other wedges" are shown in Table 3–2.) The 11 other wedges are not equally compatible with the main

Table 3–2
Entry Wedges Identified by Vesper

Types of Wedges	*Examples of the Type*
Exploiting partial momentum	Geographical transfer; supply shortage; unutilized resources
Customer sponsorship	Receipt of an advance contract; acceptance as a second source to keep pressure on an dominant supplier
Parent company sponsorship	Joint ventures or licensing; selloff of a corporate division; relinquishment of a company's market position.
Governmental sponsorship	Favored status through purchasing "set-asides" available to small or young companies; opportune timing of changes in rules or regulations governing an industry.
Combinations of wedges	

Source: Karl H. Vesper, *New Venture Strategies,* © 1980, pp. 205–233. Adapted by permission of Prentice-Hall, Inc., Englewood Cliffs, N.J.

entry wedges; in fact, Vesper identified only one (joint ventures) as being usable with a new product or service main wedge.

Vesper's concept of new venture strategy is consistent with the general concept of business strategy. He argued that high-growth potential depends on a venture's possessing a distinctive competence. Similarly, he referred to the competitive advantages that are developed through innovations and other entry wedges.

Porter and Abell also classified and described competitive strategies, each devoting specific attention to entry strategies.[100] Their works are similar enough to warrant comparison.

Porter identified three generic strategies, available to all firms regardless of age or industry. These strategies are overall cost leadership, differentiation, and focus. He used two dimensions to describe the three strategies. One, the strategic advantage, could result from product uniqueness perceived by customers or from a low cost position. The other, the strategic target, could be either industrywide or only a particular segment. Both the overall cost leadership and the differentiation strategies aim to achieve their position industrywide, whereas the focus strategy aims to achieve either low cost or perceived uniqueness within its chosen segment but not necessarily with respect to the entire industry. Research indicates that the choice of generic strategy does affect firm performance. Dess and Davis found this to be true in a fragmented industry, whereas Hall found the pursuit of either a low cost strategy or a differentiation strategy, or both, to be associated with superior company performance in eight mature industries.[101]

Abell presented a typology that appears to be quite similar to Porter's but that has crucial differences. Abell identified three alternative ways to define a business: focused strategy, differentiated strategy, and undifferentiated strategy. These strategies could be defined in terms of three measures: (1) scope; (2) differentiation of the company's offerings, one from another, across market segments; and (3) differentiation of the company's offerings from those of competitors. Both scope and differentiation should be understood in three dimensions: (1) in terms of customer groups served; (2) in terms of customer functions served; and (3) in terms of technologies utilized.[102]

Abell's *focused* strategy entails differentiation from competitors through careful tailoring of a product or service to satisfy the needs of one or a few segments. This narrow scope is based on segmentation by customer type, customer function, or technology. Similar differentiation across any or all of these three dimensions combined with a broad scope is a *differentiated* strategy. An effective basis for segmentation may be the crucial aspect of either a focused or a differentiated strategy. An *undifferentiated* strategy combines broad scope with an undifferentiated approach to customer groups, customer functions, and technology segments.

One essential difference between Porter and Abell is in their ideas of differentiation. Whereas Porter's differentiation strategy relies on the industrywide exploitation of a product's perceived uniqueness, Abell distinguishes between that form of differentiation and the competitive differentiation that results from a company's selection of a unique set of segments in which to compete. Thus Abell's differentiated strategy need not be pursued industrywide and need not rely on product differentiation within segments.

A second difference is in their treatment of the low cost position. This position is a strategy in itself, to be pursued industrywide, in Porter's scheme. Abell sees the low cost position as an objective of the undifferentiated strategy. To him, the undifferentiated strategy achieves scale economies by producing higher volumes of standardized products and/or by using standardized marketing strategies across customer groups, functions, and technologies.[103]

Both Porter and Abell treated entry strategies as special aspects of their general theories. Elaborating on his three generic strategies, Porter discussed tactics for entry through internal development by an existing firm.[104] (That his discussion dealt with an established firm rather than a new venture should not affect the validity of Porter's concepts any more than in the case of his model of industry structure.) Porter offered six generic entry concepts to overcome barriers to entry more cheaply than other firms:

Reduce product costs through process technology, economies of scale, more modern facilities, or shared activities with an existing business,

Buy in with a low price, thereby gaining share at the expense of current returns,

Offer a superior product to overcome existing differentiation,

Discover a new niche,

Introduce a marketing innovation to overcome differentiation or the power of distributors,

Use piggybacked distribution with existing products.

Abell also adopted the perspective of an existing company entering a new business.[105] He found that the implications and challenges for management differed according to the market's stage of evolution—a view that is consistent with the evolution and life-cycle literature discussed later in this chapter.

According to Abell, the pioneer in a new market typically enters with a single innovative technology designed to satisfy a particular customer function. Customers are interested more in its benefits than in its price and desire it for its own sake rather than as a part of a larger system. Customer needs and producer capabilities are unlikely to be linked closely to participation in related functions or technologies. A narrow definition of customer groups and a cream-skimming pricing policy are effective if demand is price inelastic and costs are not volume sensitive. A broad definition of customer groups and a penetration pricing policy are effective if price elasticity is high and costs are volume sensitive. Differentiation across segments is likely only if an undifferentiated approach fails to expand primary demand quickly enough.

Entry into growth markets may be based on redefinition of a business, Abell continued, most often along the dimensions of technology or customer function. Customers have become more familiar with the product and begin seeking broader applications for it and lower prices in purchasing it. Some customer groups have special needs that now are more clearly recognized. As a result, entrants in growth markets may use broad definitions aimed at attaining low costs, broad definitions aimed at selling to purchasers of entire systems, or focused or differentiated approaches aimed at satisfying special customer needs. Users of broad definitions often are larger firms able to invest the greater resources that such strategies require.

In mature or declining industries, customer behavior has changed again, Abell noted. Price weighs more heavily in purchasing decisions, but maturity also has brought more precise meeting of customer needs across functions, customer groups, and technologies. The high degree of differentiation means that the combination of broad definitions and industrywide participation is not so effective in lowering costs. A narrow definition may not entail cost disadvantages, and small firms once again are able to compete effectively. A focused approach often can be achieved through creative segmentation along one or more dimensions.

The entry strategies identified by Porter and Abell remain complementary despite the authors' somewhat different strategy definitions. Table 3–3

Table 3–3
Suitability of Porter's Entry Concepts[a] to Abell's Business Definition Strategies[b]

	Business Definition Strategies		
Entry Concepts	*Undifferentiated*	*Differentiated*	*Focused*
Reduce production costs			
New process	X		
Economies of scale	X X	X	
Production/technology improvements	X		
Buy in with a low price	X	X	X
Offer superior product		X	X
Discover segment or niche		X	X X
Marketing innovation		X X	X
Piggyback distribution	X X	X X	X

Sources: [a]Michael E. Porter, *Competitive Strategy: Techniques for Analyzing Industries and Competitors* (New York: Free Press, 1980); [b]Derek F. Abell, *Defining the Business: The Starting Point of Strategic Planning* (Englewood Cliffs, N.J.: Prentice-Hall, 1980).

Note: X X = Entry concept is highly suitable to business definition strategy; X = entry strategy is suitable to business definition strategy.

shows the apparent suitability of Porter's entry concepts to Abell's three business definition strategies.

Apart from Vesper's[106] explicit consideration of new venture strategies, the academic literature offers little on the subject. Abell[107] and Porter[108] are relevant and useful in their indirect coverage of new ventures through entry strategies. At this point in the development of new venture theory, one can say only that distinct new venture strategies seem to exist and that there is a strong theoretical basis to believe that a venture's choice of strategy affects its performance.

Literature Related to Aspects of Entrepreneurship and New Venture Performance

Several other fields of research have touched on problems and issues that are relevant to new venture performance. Treatments of such problems and issues are found in selected portions of the literature on business failure and its prediction, the performance of both independent and corporate-launched ventures, the stages of industry evolution and the product life cycle, and two special situations (the early stages of product–market evolution and strategies of low market share firms). Each of these will be covered in turn.

Business Failure and its Prediction

The quantitative study of business failure, its causes, and its prediction has been pursued vigorously for about 15 years. One review of this field concluded that most studies of company or product failure attribute 90 percent of all failures to inadequate management.[109] This estimate squares with the importance that venture capitalists and management researchers assign to "quality of management" in new ventures. Beyond this statement, though, it is difficult to apply the findings of this research to the evaluation of new ventures.

In general, the prediction of failure has been approached through the analysis of advance symptoms rather than of causes. Univariate and discriminant analyses have been applied to financial data in efforts to distinguish failed from surviving firms at some time prior to bankruptcy.[110]

The failure models could provide a rough test of a venture proposal's feasibility. That is, the venture business plan's pro forma financial statement could be used in lieu of actual data to analyze a venture's prospective probability of failure as of some future date. If the probability is high even under the typically optimistic assumptions of the business plan, the venture probably ought to be rejected. Of course such a use of the failure models probably would be more effective in disqualifying highly suspect ventures than in selecting among seemingly promising ones.

The research on predicting failure is of very limited use in evaluating new ventures. An obvious problem is the failure models' reliance on several years of financial data, which of course do not exist for new ventures. Also, most of the studies have used samples from *Moody's* or similar sources of data on medium-to-large, established corporations. Thus both age and size differ from the typical new venture. Finally, new ventures have a wide range of financial structures and vary considerably in their first-year requirements for working capital. Thus even a study of financial ratios among year-old ventures might be plagued by basically meaningless extreme values of many ratios.

Performance and Problems of New Ventures

A few studies have described the performance and problems of new ventures in ways that go beyond the survival rates discussed earlier. For the most part, though, they have examined ventures launched by corporations. The similarity of independent and corporate startups is limited. The performance of corporate startups reflects both the advantages and disadvantages of corporate sponsorship, which may include financial, political, and technological dimensions.[111] Even so, there may be room for valid comparison in the areas of competitive strategy and performance.

Biggadike performed the major study of corporate startups.[112] His sample consisted of surviving ventures launched in the late 1960s and early 1970s by "*Fortune* 200" participants in the PIMS project. Sixty-eight ventures were included, of which 47 afforded at least three or four years of data. Most were manufacturers of industrial goods and all had entered existing markets.

Median return on investment was −40 percent in the first two years and −14 percent in years three and four. Moreover, only 12 ventures reported profits in the first two years and only 18 of 47 by the end of the fourth year. None reported positive cash flows in the first two years and only 6 in years three and four.

Biggadike drew on samples of established PIMS business to estimate a period of eight years between startup and profitability and a period of 10 to 12 years from startup until returns on investment matched those of mature businesses. He projected similar delays before cash flows would turn positive or equal those of mature businesses, respectively. He cautioned that these estimates were based on the experiences of a separate sample of surviving ventures that had not necessarily shared the characteristics of his primary sample.

Biggadike found support for prior beliefs that larger market shares bring better financial performance and that share-building efforts depress financial results during the first four years. His conclusions rejected the apparent relationships of the first four years, though. Relying on other studies that demonstrated the positive correlation between market share and return on investment for PIMS businesses, Biggadike argued that a corporate venture should seek to build share "regardless of short-run financial performance" and should enter on a large scale, even building capacity in anticipation of demand.[113] Indeed, he referred to the need for large-scale entry as "the clearest recommendation from this study."[114] His data showed superior financial performance (that is, a less negative return on investment) for the upper one-third of startups when ranked by their ratio of capacity relative to market size.

American Scientific Enterprise (ASE), a management consulting firm that specialized in startups, followed Biggadike with a similar study conducted among 85 surviving startups financed by venture capital or public offerings "circa 1970."[115] Their 34 respondent firms had entered existing markets, mostly industrial. They substantially outperformed the Biggadike[116] sample on return on investment, profit-on-sales, and investment intensity measures for years two, four, and eight. Size was not beneficial: the lowest quartile (median eighth-year sales = $12 million) showed the best eighth-year median return on investment.

The ASE study lacked precise market definitions and had no data on market size or capacity relative to market size and thus could make only limited comparisons with Biggadike. Still another impediment to comparison was that both studies included only successful ventures. This meant that differences in risk exposures between corporate and independent ventures, if any existed, could be reflected only in returns to surviving ventures. Assuming that the independent ventures had higher risks, one would expect the survivors among them also to have higher returns. This could explain the superior financial performance of the ASE sample.

In summary, few conclusions can be drawn about venture performance. Despite some potential, past studies have not permitted full comparisons between corporate and independent ventures nor have they included a full range of performance outcomes.

Industry Evolution and the Product Life Cycle

The concepts of industry evolution and the product life cycle (PLC) lend dynamics to the sometimes static, and usually strategy-free, analyses of IO economists.

The PLC curve represents the unit sales or inflation-adjusted dollar sales of a product from its introduction until its demise. The curve usually is depicted as bell-shaped, although the sigmoid ascent is more widely accepted than is the shape of the descent—if indeed there is one. The marketing literature commonly divides the curve into four stages (introduction, growth, maturity, and decline), and some authors identify still more.[117] Within the past decade the PLC concept has been extended from marketing management to the broader realm of competitive strategy.[118] The strategy literature typically identifies five or more stages (for example, introduction, growth, shakeout, maturity, decline) in the PLC in order to account for changes in production, research and development, or other functional areas not usually addressed in the marketing models.

Hofer developed the theoretical argument for the PLC's role as the fundamental variable affecting the appropriateness of competitive strategies. In his later writings, he has made clear his belief that market-based and competitor-based variables drive the PLC, and not vice versa.[119]

Industry evolution poses both opportunities and threats for a business. These opportunities and threats exist in two distinct but related respects. First, the key requirements for competitive success and the types of opportunities available are likely to vary from one evolutionary stage to another. Second, the period of transition between evolutionary stages may be a time of instability, and even upheaval, in the basic structure of an industry. Because the so-called "rules of the game" and "recipes for success" are undergoing fundamental change, transition periods are times of fluidity in the relative competitive positions of industry competitors.

Hofer and Schendel described the basic stages of product–market evolution, concisely detailing their salient market, product, and process characteristics and identifying the key functional concerns of organizations during each stage.[120] They cited the development, shakeout, and decline stages of evolution as the most opportune times for firms to effect major changes in their competitive positions, as the industry leaders' customary sources of advantage may become irrelevant under the new market conditions. They also suggested generic strategies on the basis of a business unit's relative competitive position and the stage of product– market evolution.

The fundamental importance that Hofer [121] ascribed to the PLC has been subjected to some empirical examination. Anderson and Zeithaml have performed the most complete study of the PLC–strategy–performance relationship.[122] Using PIMS data on 1,234 business units during the period from 1970 to 1980, they tested for differences in the strategic determinants of high performance across the stages of the PLC. Although they concluded that the PLC was not "*the* major determinant of business strategy," Anderson and Zeithaml recommended using it as one of several contingency factors in strategy formulation.[123]

In summation, the concepts of the PLC and industry evolution (or product–market evolution, as Hofer and Schendel prefer to write) have been established as important elements in the theory of strategic management. Specifically, the effectiveness of a given business strategy varies according to the stage of evolution and the business unit's competitive position. Taken with the theoretical arguments of Abell, Porter, and Vesper concerning new venture strategies and industry entry, this means that industry evolution and/or the PLC must be considered in seeking to explain or predict new venture performance.[124]

Two Special Topics in Strategic Management

Two rather narrow topics remain to be discussed in this chapter. Both are related to the PLC concepts discussed above, but they appear to have special relevance to new ventures. The first topic is the early stages of industry evolution; the second is the strategies of low market share competitors.

Early Stages of Evolution. The advent of an industry or product form is not synonymous with new ventures but may be associated with them. Many high technology startups either originate a product or enter very early in an industry's development. Therefore the pregrowth (also called introduction, development, or precommercialization) stages of evolution warrant attention.

The major strategic variables in the introduction stage are the newness of the product, the rate of technological change in product design, buyer needs, and the product's frequency of purchase.[125] Specifically, high rates of return on investment have been associated with the importance of a product or service to its customers, high purchase frequency, and avoidance of technological change.[126]

The new industry's bases of competition often are the design, quality, and positioning of the product, although Hofer and Schendel note that price, production capacity, and access to distribution channels are more important for some types of fad products. Their recommended generic strategy is share increasing, as the firm tries to establish market dominance through heavy investment in developing and exploiting its competitive advantages.[127]

While Hofer and Schendel are apparently consistent with prior recommendations for corporate-launched ventures,[128] Anderson and Zeithaml challenged the "one strategy" notion with specific reference to the growth stage.[129] (Since the PIMS data base had only 11 introductory stage businesses, Anderson and Zeithaml could not investigate the pregrowth period.) Their data led them to recommend explicit, careful consideration of alternative strategies based on the consequences of operating at various scales over time and on the competitive and industry factors that may restrict profits during the growth stage. In effect, Anderson and Zeithaml called for managers to analyze industry structural factors rather than adhere blindly to generic prescriptions based on industry evolution.

Strategies for Low-share Competitors. Recent strategic management research on the strategic possibilities of low-share firms also has some relevance to new ventures, although the fit is imperfect. Low-share properly includes many established firms, and the research has accentuated this difference from new ventures by relying on the PIMS data base or on case histories of prominent low-share companies.[130]

Whether such research applies to new ventures depends on the validity of identifying the new venture as a low-share firm. Most industry entrants will have low shares, at least for some initial period. This would seem especially true of new ventures as opposed to diversifying large firms, since few startups command the resources necessary to achieve immediate market share prominence in an established industry.

New ventures pioneering an industry present a different situation, though. Unless an established firm enters and assumes a dominant position quite early, some new venture will have the largest share during the industry's development stage. Other new ventures may choose or fall into low-share positions during this stage. Thus low-share research has immediate relevance for many but not all new ventures in a developing industry. Over a longer period, competitive weaknesses and missed opportunities will force more of these ventures into low-share positions. Because it is desirable for firms in the early stages of industry evolution to begin developing competitive advantages to be used during the shakeout and maturity stages,[131] the prospect of becoming a low-share competitor should make these strategies relevant to most new venture managers even during an industry's development and growth stages.

Qualitative or small-sample researchers[132] have come to two points of consensus concerning low-share competitors. First, they should rely on market segmentation to exploit strengths in areas of dominant firms' weaknesses. Second, they should emphasize profitability much more than growth or market share.

Quantitative analysis of the PIMS data base led Woo to a deeper understanding of the differences between successful and unsuccessful low-share competitors.[133] She used cluster analysis of product–market–industry dimensions to create six distinct groups of businesses, then examined the strategies of effective high-share, effective low-share, and ineffective low-share businesses in each cluster. Woo found that effective and ineffective low-share businesses differed in strategies within the same clusters and that strategies were similar among successful low-share businesses in different clusters. Effective low-share businesses were not mere imitators of larger successful companies, though, as strategies differed between these two groups.

According to Woo, the successful low-share businesses selectively focused on specific strengths, tending to offer high quality and low price and spending little on marketing, research and development, or vertical integration.[134] The unsuccessful low-share firms spent more heavily for R&D, marketing, and vertical integration as they imitated the successful large-share firms by offering broad product lines. Their lower sales volumes did not support these higher overhead costs, however.

Two limitations must be acknowledged in extending Woo's conclusions to new ventures. First, as Woo pointed out, PIMS participants typically are divisions of large corporations and therefore enjoy advantages and face constraints that are not found among independent low-share businesses. Second, the unsuccessful low-share businesses may not have intended to have low shares. If resource sufficiency encourages an entrant to seek dominance, then one would expect divisions of large corporations to choose a high-share strategy more frequently than would small or new companies. Given the divisional status and presumed resource sufficiency of most PIMS participants, it seems likely that the poor performance of low-share businesses arose not from their current strategies so much as from their past failures to execute those (or other) strategies. Woo's data were in static, cross-sectional form, which raises the possibility that the observed current strategies of unsuccessful low-share businesses were residuals of their failed drives for high market share rather than plans formulated with low-share competition in mind. Alternatively, observed strategies could represent recent responses to the unacceptable results of past strategies. Results would be expected to lag strategic changes, but cross-sectional research could mistakenly associate the results with the observed current strategy. It is regrettable that PIMS cannot register intentions as well as performance data and offers only limited potential for longitudinal research.

Regardless of the limitations of Woo's research, a consensus emerges from this area of inquiry. Each cited work highlighted the importance of segmentation, specialization, and the selective development of competences. This supports the prescriptions for segmentation, focus, and differentiation described in the business strategy portion of this review.

Summary of the Related Literature

In general, the related literature has been consistent with the literature on entrepreneurship and new venture performance reviewed earlier. Drawing on the diverse topics grouped in this section, several observations can be made.

The quantitative research on new venture performance provided important insights. Biggadike's[135] strong endorsement of large-scale entry and ambitious share objectives may reflect the nature of the industrial goods markets or of corporate sponsorship, but his study had another implication for research on new venture strategy. The corporate ventures in his sample displayed strategy–performance relationships much like those of their PIMS parents. If corporate ventures are subject to the same strategic "laws" as the corporations that launch them, then the contingency theories of strategy could apply to independent new ventures as well as to the established firms on whose performance the theories were based. This strengthens the argument for considering new ventures as a special case of the general theories of strategy, which is the approach taken in this book.

The States of Theory and Research Compared

This book's attempt to draw on several fields in building a model of new venture performance encounters major differences among the fields in their progress in understanding and measuring relevant variables. These differences reflect the different states of theory and research on venture business strategy, industry structural characteristics, and the characteristics of entrepreneurs.

Descriptive theory and research characterize some parts of the field of strategic management, whereas prescriptive theory and normative research are more common in others. Descriptive theories tell "what is" for their domain; prescriptive theories tell what will occur if certain actions are taken.

Prescriptive theories therefore must contain at least one variable subject to management's control.[136]

Descriptive research and theory fulfill ontological requirements of normative research by exploring and mapping territory, which permits hypothesis generation. Once a territory is more thoroughly mapped it may be possible to develop several limited-domain theories out of what previously had appeared to be an atheoretic jumble of conflicting tendencies.

The combination of limited-domain theories to cover an entire territory yields a contingency theory. Insofar as is possible, such contingency theories should be developed from well-corroborated limited-domain theories.[137] The researcher who seeks to integrate theories from related disciplines faces similar requirements and obstacles.

Most research on entrepreneurial characteristics has taken a descriptive, empiricist approach. Using concrete data on entrepreneurs' educations, family backgrounds, experience, and more, researchers have attempted to correlate entrepreneurial success with various personal characteristics. Despite some success in profiling entrepreneurs and somewhat less success in distinguishing them from the general population, the psychological research has developed almost no *ex ante* distinctions between successful and unsuccessful entrepreneurs.[138] Less quantitative research has yielded similar results.[139] Biographical data have yielded clearer distinctions between successful and failed entrepreneurs,[140] from which has emerged a consensus identifying several types of experience as important factors in entrepreneurial performance.

Although some theory testing has been done in this area, research on the determinants of success remains in the theory-building stage. Part of the problem appears to be the failure of researchers to identify all key variables affecting performance. Thus researchers are left to explain conflicting findings of individual studies without recourse to a fuller model of entrepreneurial and new venture performance.

Comparisons of new venture performance between sectors of the economy have rested on rates of survival in different lines of business. Such research, too, has taken a descriptive, empiricist approach. Unlike some studies of the psychology and experience of entrepreneurs, these comparisons have made little use of a priori logic. Mortality rates typically are compared and differences noted, with little theoretical explanation.[141] The value of such studies is limited by the inadequate foundations for comparison across studies. It should be noted, too, that in the absence of theory grounded in a priori logic concerning industry structure, the value of empirical studies of any sector at any particular time must be unique and evanescent.

IO economists traditionally emphasized structure, even to the exclusion of firm conduct variables from IO models. Scherer and other behaviorists have added firms' actions and strategies to more recent IO models.[142] The behaviorists' ontological departure from the structuralist paradigm has eased the task of integrating theories of IO and strategic management. The well-known competitive strategy approach of Michael Porter applies theoretical frameworks and assumptions from both fields to the types of data that interest scholars in both fields.[143]

The competitive strategy approach is decidely less empiricist than the research on entrepreneurial characteristics. Applications of this approach have used interpretive analysis more frequently and readily than empiricism,[144] although more recent work has moved toward a combination of methods.[145] Hofer and Schendel's prescriptive theory[146] resembles the competitive strategy approach in its essential rationality and nonempiricism, despite differences described elsewhere.[147] Both Porter and Hofer and Schendel represent a different view of strategic management than the PIMS-based studies.[148] The latter[149] epitomize empiricism; in fact, the empirically derived regression model has been called the "ontological heart" of PIMS.[150]

Prescriptive theory springing from PIMS research rests on a logic of imitation rather than on logical constructions from prior foundations. PIMS-based research has been static and cross-sectional, yielding statistically verifiable statements about correlations but relatively tenuous statements about causation. Research based on the Porter or Hofer–Schendel approaches typically is more definite about cause than in its statistical power.[151] Neither the PIMS nor the alternative approaches has produced fully explicated, corroborated theory.[152]

Applications of strategic management theory to new ventures has not advanced even to the state of research on competitive strategy. Theory relating specifically to new venture strategy appears to be nonexistent except for the work of Vesper, whose efforts have been in exploration and concept development.[153] His contribution has been his identification and description of new venture strategies.

New venture strategy is the least researched and least developed of the three fields under consideration here. The state of theory and research in new venture strategy necessarily restricts the researcher who would model the determinants of new venture performance or develop theories of new venture performance and entrepreneurship. The researcher building a theory of new venture performance thus is driven to using the slightly more developed theories concerning entrepreneurial characteristics and industry structure to identify potentially critical variables that might join or affect venture business strategy in predicting venture performance.

In chapter 4 these three fields are combined to describe the conceptual framework that guides academic thought on new venture performance. This framework will be contrasted to a *practitioner framework* developed from venture capitalists' wisdom. The two frameworks will be synthesized to create a new conceptual framework of new venture performance.

Summary

This chapter has drawn on both economics and management literature for its conception of the entrepreneur. From economists, and from the Austrian school in particular, come the differences in knowledge, perception, ignorance, and error that cause similarly motivated people to respond differently to a given situation. The entrepreneur who possesses superior insights or foresight, correctly identifies or anticipates economic disequilibrium and exploits it. The entrepreneur whose insights prove incorrect and whose foresight proves faulty directs investment in ways that eventually prove inappropriate. Right or wrong in his or her expectations and actions, the entrepreneur invariably operates in an environment of risk and uncertainty.

The management literature reminds us that the entrepreneur is more than the humanized calculator portrayed in static-state equilibrium analyses. The entrepreneur makes necessary compromises between conflicting objectives and sometimes prefers leisure or self-employment to financial returns. Only some entrepreneurs commence their ventures with any intention of having them become large.

The entrepreneur as conceived here is one who engages in purposeful activity undertaken to initiate, maintain, and aggrandize a profit-oriented business unit. The entrepreneur hopes his or her perception of an exploitable disequilibrium is accurate (or comes to pass) and that the venture becomes profitable and viable at its maturity. This conception of the entrepreneur excludes the founder of the intendedly marginal firm.

Entrepreneur and venture exist in a competitive environment in which numerous factors affect performance. The most directly significant and individually variable factors are grouped under three subject headings: characteristics of the entrepreneur, characteristics of the industry, and venture business strategy.

The most fundamental conclusions of this review of the literature were summarized in table 1–1. They were supported and elaborated by a review of the literature concerning related aspects of business failure and its prediction, the performance of both corporate and independent new ventures, the stages of industry evolution and the product life cycle, and the strategies of low market share businesses.

The final portion of this chapter compared the states of theory and research in three key areas. It was found that theory-building research is still necessary in the area of new venture strategy because only exploration and concept development have been undertaken in the past. The only slightly more advanced research on entrepreneurial characteristics and industry structure as related to new venture performance are of value in identifying, and perhaps in measuring, variables that could join or affect strategy in determining new venture performance.

Notes

1. Dolores Tremewan Martin, "Alternative Views of Mengerian Entrepreneurship," *History of Political Economy* 11 (1979):271.
2. Ludwig von Mises, *Human Action,* 3rd rev. ed. (Chicago: Henry Regnery Company, 1966), p. 252.
3. Israel M. Kirzner, *Perception, Opportunity, and Profit* (Chicago: University of Chicago Press, 1979).
4. Martin, "Alternative Views," p. 275.
5. Frank H. Knight, *Risk, Uncertainty and Profit* (Boston: Houghton Mifflin, 1921), p.268.
6. Knight, *Risk, Uncertainty and Profit.*
7. Joseph A. Schumpeter, *The Theory of Economic Development* (Cambridge, Mass.: Harvard University Press, 1934), p. 74.
8. Ibid., pp. 93–94.
9. Ibid., p. 137.
10. Kirzner, *Perception, Opportunity, and Profit,* p. 110.
11. Carl Menger, *Principles of Economics,* translated by James Dingwall and Bert F. Hoselitz (New York: New York University Press, 1981).
12. Ibid.
13. Mises, *Human Action,* p. 585.
14. Ibid.
15. Edith Tilton Penrose, *The Theory of the Growth of the Firm* (New York: John Wiley & Sons, 1959).
16. Frederick Arthur Webster, "Entrepreneurs and Ventures: An Attempt at Classification and Clarification," *Academy of Management Review* 2 (1977):54–61.
17. Patrick R. Liles, *New Business and the Entrepreneur* (Homewood, Ill.: Richard D. Irwin, 1974), p. 4.
18. Jeffrey Susbauer, "Commentary," in *Strategic Management,* edited by Dan E. Schendel and Charles W. Hofer (Boston: Little, Brown, 1979), pp. 327–332.
19. James W. Carland, Frank Hoy, William R. Boulton, and Jo Ann C. Carland, "Differentiating Entrepreneurs from Small Business Owners: A Conceptualization," *Academy of Management Review* 9 (1984):354–359.
20. In other words, they may be "unconscious underachievers" but are unlikely to be "conscious underachievers" as Susbauer ("Commentary") used the terms.
21. Karl H. Vesper has categorized and summarized this literature. See his "Commentary," in *Strategic Management*, edited by Dan E. Schendel and Charles W. Hofer (Boston: Little, Brown, 1979), pp. 332–338, and his *New Venture Strategies* (Englewood Cliffs, N. J.: Prentice-Hall, 1980).
22. Arnold C. Cooper, "Strategic Management: New Ventures and Small Business," in *Strategic Management,* edited by Dan E. Schendel and Charles W. Hofer (Boston: Little, Brown, 1979), pp. 316–327.
23. Robert Buchele, *Business Policy in Growing Firms* (Scranton, Pa.: Chandler Publishing Company, 1967), p. 17.
24. William M. Hoad and Peter Rosko, *Management Factors Contributing to the Success and Failure of New Small Manufacturers* (Ann Arbor, Mich.: Bureau of Business Research, University of Michigan, 1964).

25. Orvis F. Collins and David G. Moore, *The Enterprising Man* (East Lansing, Mich.: Michigan State University, 1964).
26. Norman Raymond Smith, *The Entrepreneur and His Firm: The Relationship Between Type of Man and Type of Company* (East Lansing, Mich.: Bureau of Business and Economic Research, Michigan State University, 1967).
27. Arnold C. Cooper, *The Founding of Technology-based Firms* (Milwaukee, Wis.: The Center for Venture Management, 1971).
28. Buchele, *Business Policy in Growing Firms.*
29. Smith, *Entrepreneur and His Firm.*
30. Hoad and Rosko, *Success and Failure.*
31. Ibid., p. 93. These data are analyzed in William R. Sandberg, "The Determinants of New Venture Performance: Strategy, Industry Structure and Entrepreneur," Ph.D. diss., Athens, Ga.: The University of Georgia, 1984, pp. 78–79.
32. Buchele, *Business Policy in Growing Firms.*
33. Hoad and Rosko, *Success and Failure.*
34. Cooper, *Founding of Technology-based Firms.*
35. Edward B. Roberts, "A Basic Study of Innovators; How to Keep and Capitalize on Their Talents," *Research Management* 11 (1968):249–266.
36. Buchele, *Business Policy in Growing Firms,* p. 20.
37. Hoad and Rosko, *Success and Failure.* The data are analyzed by Sandberg, "Determinants of New Venture Performance," pp. 78–81.
38. Smith, *Entrepreneur and His Firm.*
39. Collins and Moore, *Enterprising Man,* p. 80.
40. Lawrence M. Lamont, "What Entrepreneurs Learn From Experience," *Journal of Small Business Management* 10 (July 1972):36–41.
41. John A. Hornaday and John Aboud, "Characteristics of Successful Entrepreneurs," *Personnel Psychology* 24 (1971):141–153; Merrill E. Douglass, "Relating Education to Entrepreneurial Success," *Business Horizons* 19 (December 1976):40–44; Donald L. Sexton, "Characteristics and Role Demands of Successful Entrepreneurs," paper presented to the Academy of Management, Detroit, August 1980; Arnold C. Cooper and William C. Dunkelberg, "Influences Upon Entrepreneurship—A Large-Scale Study," paper presented to the Academy of Management, San Diego, August 1981.
42. Robert H. Brockhaus and W. R. Nord, "An Exploration of the Factors Affecting the Entrepreneurial Decision: Personal Characteristics vs. Environmental Conditions," *Proceedings, Academy of Management,* 1979, pp. 364–368; Cooper and Dunkelberg, "Influences Upon Entrepreneurship."
43. Douglass, "Relating Education to Entrepreneurial Success."
44. Carl M. Larson and Ronald C. Clute, "The Failure Syndrome," *American Journal of Small Business* 4 (October 1974):35–43.
45. Hoad and Rosko, *Success and Failure,* p. 10.
46. Ibid., p. 11.
47. Cooper, *Technology-based Firms.*
48. Roberts, "Innovators."
49. George H. Litwin and Robert A. Stringer, *Motivation and Organizational Climate* (Boston: Division of Research, Harvard University, 1968), p. 12.
50. David C. McClelland, *The Achieving Society* (Princeton, N.J.: D. Van Nostrand, 1961).

51. David C. McClelland, "N Achievement and Entrepreneurship: A Longitudinal Study," *Journal of Personality and Social Psychology* 1 (1965):389–392.

52. Hornaday and Aboud, "Characteristics of Successful Entrepreneurs;" John L. Komives, "A Preliminary Study of the Personal Values of High-Technology Entrepreneurs," in *Technical Entrepreneurship: A Symposium,* edited by Arnold C. Cooper and John L. Komives (Milwaukee, Wis.: The Center for Venture Management, 1972).

53. McClelland, "N Achievement and Entrepreneurship;" David C. McClelland and David G. Winter, *Motivating Economic Achievement* (New York: Free Press, 1969).

54. Jeffry A. Timmons, "Black is Beautiful—Is It Bountiful?" *Harvard Business Review* 49 (November 1971): 81–94.

55. Jeffry A. Timmons, "Motivating Economic Achievement: A Five Year Appraisal," *Proceedings of the Fifth Annual Meeting* (Boston, 1973), American Institute of Decision Sciences.

56. Harry Schrage, "The R&D Entrepreneur: Profile of Success," *Harvard Business Review* 43 (November 1965):56–69.

57. Herbert A. Wainer and Irwin M. Rubin, "Motivation of Research and Development Entrepreneurs," *Journal of Applied Psychology* 53 (1969):178–184.

58. Hornaday and Aboud, "Characteristics of Successful Entrepreneurs;" Robert H. Brockhaus, "Psychology of the Entrepreneur," paper presented at the Conference on Research and Education in Entrepreneurship, St. Louis University, March 24–25, 1980.

59. J. B. Rotter, "Generalized Expectancies for Internal Versus External Control of Reinforcement," *Psychological Monographs: General and Applied,* 80, no. 1, Whole No. 609, 1966.

60. Liles, *New Business and the Entrepreneur.*

61. Robert H. Brockhaus, "I-E Locus of Control Scores as Predictors of Entrepreneurial Intentions," paper presented to the Academy of Management, New Orleans, 1975.

62. Albert Shapero, "The Displaced, Uncomfortable Entrepreneur," *Psychology Today* (November 1975):83–89.

63. Brockhaus and Nord, "Factors Affecting the Entrepreneurial Decision"; Timothy Scott Mescon, "Entrepreneurship in the Real Estate Industry: A Comparative Analysis of Independent and Franchise Brokers," Ph.D. diss., Athens, Ga.: University of Georgia, 1979.

64. Robert H. Brockhaus, "Psychological and Environmental Factors Which Distinguish the Successful from the Unsuccessful Entrepreneur: A Longitudinal Study," *Proceedings, Academy of Management,* 1980, pp. 368–372.

65. Liles, *New Business and the Entrepreneur.*

66. McClelland, *The Achieving Society*; Joseph Mancuso, "The Entrepreneur's Quiz," in *The Entrepreneur's Handbook 2,* edited by Joseph Mancuso (Dedham, Mass.: Artech House, 1974) pp. 235–239; Mescon, "Entrepreneurship in the Real Estate Industry"; Sexton, "Characteristics and Role Demands of Successful Entrepreneurs."

67. Robert H. Brockhaus, "Risk-Taking Propensity of Entrepreneurs," *Academy of Management Journal* 23 (1980):509–520.

68. Brockhaus, "Psychological and Environmental Factors."

69. Brockhaus, "Psychology of the Entrepreneur," p. 9.

70. Hoad and Rosko, *Success and Failure.*

71. For example, Collins and Moore, *Enterprising Man,* and Vesper, *New Venture Strategies.*

72. Vesper, *New Venture Strategies,* p. 29.

73. Hoad and Rosko, *Success and Failure.*

74. Vesper, *New Venture Strategies,* p. 29.

75. F. M. Scherer, *Industrial Market Structure and Economic Performance* (Chicago: Rand McNally, 1970).

76. For an explanation of how the IO paradigm began to penetrate the strategic management literature, see Michael E. Porter, "The Contributions of Industrial Organization to Strategic Management," *Academy of Management Review* 6 (1981):609–620.

77. Michael E. Porter, *Competitive Strategy* (New York: Free Press, 1980).

78. Ibid.

79. Schumpeter, *Theory of Economic Development.*

80. Kirzner, *Perception, Opportunity, and Profit.*

81. For example, see Porter, "Contributions of Industrial Organization"; John E. Prescott, "The Development of an Industry Typology," paper presented to the Academy of Management, San Diego, 1981.

82. Porter, "Contributions of Industrial Organization."

83. For example, see Carolyn Y. Y. Woo, "Strategies for Low Market Share Businesses," Ph.D. diss., West Lafayette, Ind.: Purdue University, 1980; Kathryn Rudie Harrigan, *Strategies for Vertical Integration* (Lexington, Mass.: Lexington Books, 1983).

84. George S. Yip, *Barriers to Entry: A Corporate-Strategy Perspective* (Lexington, Mass.: Lexington Books, 1982).

85. The PIMS data base contains market and firm data supplied in confidence by participants in the Profit Impact of Marketing Strategy (PIMS) research of the Strategic Planning Institute. These participants are business units of very large corporations, engaged primarily in manufacturing industrial goods. For a critique of this data base and its research uses, see Carl R. Anderson and Frank I. Paine, "PIMS: A Reexamination," *Academy of Management Review* 3 (1978):602–612.

86. Porter, *Competitive Strategy.*

87. William Gartner, "Entry Strategies in an Emerging Industry," *Proceedings, Academy of Management,* 1983, pp. 413–416.

88. Vesper, *New Venture Strategies.*

89. Porter, *Competitive Strategy.*

90. Porter, "Contributions of Industrial Organization."

91. Dan E. Schendel and Charles W. Hofer, eds., *Strategic Management* (Boston: Little, Brown, 1979).

92. Charles W. Hofer, "Toward a Contingency Theory of Business Strategy," *Academy of Management Journal* 18 (1975):784–810.

93. Charles W. Hofer and Dan E. Schendel, *Strategy Formulation: Analytical Concepts* (St. Paul, Minn.: West Publishing Co., 1978).

94. Hofer, "Toward a Contingency Theory."

95. For example, see Kenneth J. Hatten, "Strategic Models in the Brewing In-

dustry," Ph.D. diss., West Lafayette, Ind.: Purdue University, 1974; Kathryn Rudie Harrigan, *Strategies for Declining Businesses* (Lexington, Mass.: Lexington Books, 1980); Woo, "Strategies for Low Market Share Businesses"; and William R. Soukup, "Strategic Responses to Technological Threats," Ph.D. diss., West Lafayette, Ind.: Purdue University, 1979.

96. Hofer and Schendel, *Strategy Formulation.*

97. Derek F. Abell, *Defining the Business: The Starting Point of Strategic Planning* (Englewood Cliffs, N.J.: Prentice-Hall, 1980), pp. 22–23.

98. Cooper, "Strategic Management."

99. Vesper, *New Venture Strategies.*

100. Porter, *Competitive Strategy;* Abell, *Defining the Business.*

101. Gregory G. Dess and Peter S. Davis, "Porter's (1980) Generic Strategies as Determinants of Strategic Group Membership and Organizational Performance," *Academy of Management Journal* 27 (1984):467–488; William K. Hall, "Survival Strategies in a Hostile Environment," *Harvard Business Review* 58 (September 1980):75–85.

102. Abell, *Defining the Business.*

103. Porter's more recent treatment of generic strategies recognizes more explicitly the tradeoffs against differentiation that may be required by an industrywide low-cost position. See Michael E. Porter, *Competitive Advantage* (New York: Free Press, 1985).

104. Porter, *Competitive Strategy.*

105. Abell, *Defining the Business.*

106. Vesper, *New Venture Strategies.*

107. Abell, *Defining the Business.*

108. Porter, *Competitive Strategy.*

109. Subhash Sharma and Vijay Mahajan, "Early Warning Indicators of Business Failure," *Journal of Marketing* 44 (1980):80–89.

110. W. H. Beaver, "Financial Ratios as Predictors of Failure," *Empirical Research in Accounting: Selected Studies,* Supplement to *Journal of Accounting Research* 4 (1966):71–111; Edward I. Altman, "Financial Ratios, Discriminant Analysis and the Prediction of Corporate Bankruptcy," *Journal of Finance* 23 (1968):589–609; Sharma and Mahajan, "Early Warning Indicators."

111. Richard M. Hill and James D. Hlavacek, "Learning from Failure: Ten Guidelines for Venture Management," *California Management Review* 19 (Summer 1977):5–16; Norman D. Fast, *The Rise and Fall of Corporate New Venture Divisions* (Ann Arbor, Mich.: UMI Research Press, 1978); Robert A. Burgelman, "Managing Innovating Systems: A Study of the Process of Internal Corporate Ventures," Ph.D diss., New York: Columbia University, 1980.

112. E. Ralph Biggadike, *Corporate Diversification: Entry, Strategy, and Performance* (Boston: Graduate School of Business, Harvard University, 1979).

113. Ralph Biggadike, "The Risky Business of Diversification," *Harvard Business Review* 57 (May 1979):108.

114. Biggadike, "Risky Business," p. 110.

115. American Scientific Enterprise, Inc., *Startup Business—The Offensive Side of the Game* (Great Neck, N.Y.: American Scientific Enterprise, 1980).

116. Biggadike, *Corporate Diversification.*

117. David R. Rink and John E. Swan, "Product Life Cycle Research: A Literature Review," *Journal of Business Research* 87 (1979):219–242.

118. For example, by Chester Wasson, *Dynamic Competitive Strategy and Product Life Cycles* (St. Charles, Ill.: Challenge Books, 1974); Hofer, "Toward a Contingency Theory"; Charles W. Hofer, "Conceptual Constructs for Formulating Corporate and Business Strategies," Boston: Intercollegiate Case Clearing House, 9–378–754, 1977; Pater Patel and Michael Younger, "A Frame of Reference for Strategy Development," *Long-Range Planning* 11 (April 1978):6–12.

119. Charles W. Hofer, "Product–Market Fundamentals vs. the Product Life Cycle," paper presented at the Conference on Nontraditional Approaches to Policy Research, Los Angeles, University of Southern California, November, 1981.

120. Hofer and Schendel, *Strategy Formulation.*

121. Hofer, "Toward a Contingency Theory."

122. Carl R. Anderson and Carl P. Zeithaml, "Stage of Product Life Cycle, Business Strategy, and Business Performance," *Academy of Management Journal* 27 (1984):5–24.

123. Ibid., p. 22. Emphasis in the original.

124. Abell, *Defining the Business*; Porter, *Competitive Strategy*; Vesper, *New Venture Strategies.*

125. Hofer, "Toward a Contingency Theory."

126. Anderson and Zeithaml, "Stage of the Product Life Cycle."

127. Hofer and Schendel, *Strategy Formulation.*

128. Biggadike, *Corporate Diversification.*

129. Anderson and Zeithaml, "Stage of the Product Life Cycle."

130. As noted earlier, the PIMS data base consists of large businesses that are units of major corporations. Even research users of the data point out that PIMS participants "probably are more sophisticated, more dominant within their markets, and more effective in general" than the typical business (Donald C. Hambrick, Ian C. MacMillan, Diana L. Day, "Strategic Attributes and Performance in the BCG Matrix—A PIMS-Based Analysis of Industrial Products Businesses," *Academy of Management Journal* 25 [1982]:510–531).

131. Hofer and Schendel, *Strategy Formulation.*

132. For example, Richard G. Hamermesh, M. J. Anderson, Jr., and M. E. Harris, "Strategies for Low Market Share Businesses," *Harvard Business Review* 56 (May 1978):95–102; Ronald Stiff and Inder Khera, "Strategies for Low Market-Share Companies," *Applied Business and Administration Quarterly* 1 (Spring 1981):8–12.

133. Woo, "Strategies for Low Market Share Businesses"; Carolyn Y. Y. Woo and Arnold Cooper, "Strategies of Effective Low Share Businesses," *Strategic Management Journal* 2 (1981):301–318.

134. The low level of R&D spending contradicts the findings of Hamermesh, Anderson, and Harris, "Strategies for Low Market Share Businesses."

135. Biggadike, *Corporate Diversification.*

136. Schendel and Hofer, eds., *Strategic Management.*

137. Ibid., p. 392.

138. Brockhaus, "Psychological and Environmental Factors" and "Psychology of the Entrepreneur."

139. For example, Collins and Moore, *Enterprising Man.*

140. For example, Hoad and Rosko, *Success and Failure.*

141. For example, Vesper, *New Venture Strategies.*

142. Scherer, *Industrial Market Structure and Economic Performance.*

143. Porter, *Competitive Strategy.*

144. For example, see Harrigan, *Strategies for Declining Businesses,* and her somewhat extended interpretation in "Strategies for Declining Industries," *Journal of Business Strategy* 1 (Fall 1980):20–34. See also Porter, *Competitive Strategy.*

145. The research of Harrigan herself has evolved in this direction. See for example, Kathryn Rudie Harrigan, "Deterrents to Divestiture," *Academy of Management Journal* 24 (1981):306–323; also Kathryn Rudie Harrigan, *Strategies for Vertical Integration* (Lexington, Mass.: Lexington Books, 1983); Kathryn Rudie Harrigan, "Research Methodologies for Contingency Approaches to Business Strategy," *Academy of Management Review* 8 (1983):398–405. See also Yip, *Barriers to Entry.*

146. Hofer and Schendel, *Strategy Formulation.*

147. Ian I. Mitroff and Richard O. Mason, "Business Policy and Metaphysics: Some Philosophical Considerations," *Academy of Management Review* 7 (1982):361–371.

148. Porter, *Competitive Strategy;* Hofer and Schendel, *Strategy Formulation.*

149. For example, Biggadike, *Corporate Diversification;* Hambrick, Macmillan, and Day, "Strategic Attributes and Performance in the BCG Matrix"; Hatten, "Strategic Models in the Brewing Industry"; Ian C. MacMillan, Donald C. Hambrick, and Diana L. Day, "The Product Portfolio and Profitability—A PIMS-Based Analysis of Industrial-Product Businesses," *Academy of Management Journal* 25 (1982):733–755; Woo, "Strategies for Low Market Share Businesses."

150. Mitroff and Mason, "Business Policy and Metaphysics," p. 364.

151. Porter, *Competitive Strategy;* Hofer and Schendel, *Strategy Formulation.*

152. For a discussion of the methodological issues that confront strategic management research and a proposed hybrid methodology to resolve them, see Harrigan, "Research Methodologies for Contingency Approaches."

153. Vesper, *New Venture Strategies.*

4 New Venture Performance: A Conceptual Framework

Previous chapters have explored the wisdom of venture capitalists and the theory and research of academics as they concern new venture performance. From practitioners came the justification for broadening the scope of inquiry beyond the characteristics of the entrepreneur—which have been the typical focus of research—to include elements of strategy and industry structure. Chapter 3 reviewed and integrated theory and research from these three areas.

Chapter 4 presents a new conceptual framework, or model, of new venture performance. In it I pose the questions and develop the propositions that were tested in the research for this book. The chapter begins with a comparison of the academic and practitioner frameworks of new venture performance that were identified, developed, and described in the preceding chapters. These two frameworks differ in orientation and measurement, but they offer grounds for a useful synthesis. This new conceptual framework synthesizes the academic and practitioner frameworks and corrects their omissions. The new framework's dependent variables represent the performance of the new venture; its independent variables represent the characteristics of the entrepreneur, the industry structure, and the venture business strategy. The new framework suggests the following relationship: $NVP = f(E, IS, S)$.

Following the exposition of this new framework are this book's research questions. Each question is stated along with its basis in existing theory and research. Finally, the 19 propositions that will be tested in this research are stated and justified through theoretical arguments.

Comparison of the Academic and Practitioner Frameworks

The two preceding chapters have addressed entrepreneurship and new venture performance from two different perspectives. Chapter 2 drew on both literature and interviews to present the thoughts and practices of venture capitalists with respect to new venture evaluation. Chapter 3 reviewed and interpreted the academic literature and assessed the states of theory and research on these and related topics.

To better understand and compare how these two perspectives address entrepreneurship and new venture performance, I constructed conceptual frameworks for them. The conceptual frameworks described how each perspective treats the relationships between three key factors (characteristics of the entrepreneur, characteristics of the industry, and venture business strategy) and new venture performance. In the following pages the *academic framework* and the *practitioner framework* will be compared in terms of their inclusiveness, their measurements, and the strength and thoroughness of their conclusions. These comparisons are summarized in table 4–1.

Inclusiveness

The characteristics of the entrepreneur are covered extensively in the academic literature but generally are not associated with venture performance. As Brockhaus has noted, psychological variables have not been related to entrepreneurial success or failure.[1] The entrepreneur's experience is a significant factor in the academic framework of new venture performance, though.[2]

The academic framework includes sector-of-the-economy as a factor in comparisons across surveys but rarely within any one study. Industry structure has traditionally been omitted. The framework includes venture business strategy through a handful of theoretical and conceptual works, but has rarely related strategy to venture performance.[3]

The practitioner framework is more inclusive with respect to the three factors of entrepreneurial characteristics, industry characteristics, and venture business strategy. Both the experience and the psychology of the entrepreneur play major parts in the venture capitalist's evaluation of a new venture. Unlike the academic framework, the practitioner framework has a pragmatic emphasis in its consideration of the entrepreneur's characteristics. The venture capitalist is much less interested in what prompted the entrepreneurial act than in how a venture will perform.

Industry structure figured in the criteria used by the interviewed venture capitalists. Fragmented industries were considered relatively attractive, although other factors weighed more heavily. Venture capitalists also expressed preferences for sectors of the economy, but these preferences usually reflected a venture capitalist's knowledge or experience as much as an assessment of sector attractiveness. Finally, the practitioner framework includes venture business strategy and relates it to performance.

Table 4–1
Comparisons of Academic and Practitioner Models of New Venture Performance

Characteristics of	*Academic Model*	*Practitioner Model*
Inclusiveness of the Model		
Entrepreneur	Extensive coverage but only sometimes related to performance	Definitely included; pragmatic performance orientation
Industry structure	Not directly addressed in entrepreneurship research	Included; sometimes related to performance but often to venture capitalist's expertise
Strategy	Included in a few theoretical and conceptual works	Included, related to performance
Measurement of Variables		
Entrepreneur	Quantitative, objective	Qualitative, subjective for psychological personality variables
Industry structure	Objective and nominal sector identification; structure not covered	Qualitative assessment of industry structure
Strategy	Qualitative, subjective	Qualitative, subjective
Thoroughness of Conclusions		
Entrepreneur	Psychological: limited; experience: fairly thorough	Thorough, somewhat contingent
Industry structure	Extremely limited	Quite limited
Strategy	Extremely limited	Limited, noncontingent

Measurement

As might be expected from their different backgrounds and objectives, academics and practitioners rely on different types of measurement in their frameworks of new venture performance. The academic framework uses quantitative, objective data on the entrepreneur's characteristics far more frequently than does the practitioner framework. None of the interviewed venture capitalists administered or used the results of psychological tests, for example. Their approach was more intuitive, relying on their feel for a person's qualities. The measurement of an entrepreneur's experience presents a similar but smaller difference: Academics generally have used "number of years," whereas practitioners have used the more qualitative "track record," which blends objective experience with a subjective performance appraisal.

Measurement of industry structure is irrelevant to the academic framework, since it is omitted as a factor. Structure figures in venture capitalists' evaluations of new ventures, but its measurement is not articulated other than by qualitative labeling of ventures' industries.

Both academics and practitioners measure venture business strategies, and both rely on nominal measures. There is considerable subjectivity involved in identifying and describing the strategies. In this regard, both frameworks probably reflect the inability of the parent field of business policy to measure strategy more precisely.

Thoroughness of Conclusions

The conclusions to be found in either framework are limited. Only the entrepreneur's characteristics have been linked at all closely to performance. Experience, particularly when qualified as to type or duration, has been related to performance more thoroughly than any other factor in the academic framework. The same is true of the practitioner framework, with the latter's added subjectivity yielding possible stronger conclusions. The thoroughness of the academic framework's conclusions concerning the psychological variables generally exceeds their strength, at least with respect to new venture performance.

Neither framework offers many conclusions, apart from those concerning the characteristics of entrepreneurs. The academic framework identifies venture business strategies but has not associated them with performance. Practitioners proclaim definite strategic preferences, but their framework is limited by the unarticulated, noncontingent nature of most of those preferences.

Summary of Comparisons

The tenor of the practitioner framework is pragmatic, whereas that of the academic framework is scholarly; hence the practitioner framework's greater reliance on subjective and qualitative measurements and greater orientation toward predicting performance. Academics have proceeded slowly, if indeed a theory of new venture performance (as distinguished from initiation) has been their aim. They have developed useful classification schemes and strategic concepts that are absent from the practitioner framework, but their implicit theory of new venture performance has been $NVP = f(E)$. Despite its roughness, the practitioner framework suggests a richer theory: $NVP = f(E, IS, S)$. At this time the possibilities for synthesis lie in adding the practitioners' richness and performance orientation to the mapping and classification efforts of the academics. This undertaking begins with the presentation of a new, synthesized framework of new venture performance.

A New Framework of New Venture Performance

This framework (or conceptual model) of new venture performance is intended to provide an analytic framework and to generate propositions to be examined and tested. Following the literature's major research path and venture capitalists' main basis for investment decisions, it includes characteristics of the entrepreneur. But it also is intended to close the gap in new venture research that results from the failure to include strategy when studying performance. This framework includes competitive strategy as an independent variable, thereby following the practice of the strategic management literature. Industry structure and evolution are other important additions that set this framework apart from other new venture research. The importance of industry structure and evolution in economic and strategic management theory and research prompt their inclusion here.

The relationships denoted by $NVP = f(E, IS, S)$ represent an essentially new paradigm of new venture performance. The empirical portion of this study was intended to illuminate these relationships. The entrepreneur, industry structure, and new venture strategy had to be defined in terms of variables, and those variables required classification schemes or some other basis for comparison between ventures. These tasks are taken up next. Each of the three areas of interest will be described, traced to its origins in the literature and in venture capitalists' practices, and defined for the purposes of this book. (The variables and categories that compose the framework are listed in table 4–2.) Following the discussion of the independent variables, new venture performance is also discussed and defined.

Characteristics of the Entrepreneur

The characteristics of the entrepreneur include prior entrepreneurial and startup experience, managerial experience in related industries, age, and education. Each has support in the academic literature and among venture capitalists.

Prior entrepreneurial performance is a primary criterion used by the interviewed venture capitalists. Like venture capitalists in general, they valued successful experience in any entrepreneurial role about as highly as managerial experience in a relevant industry. The academic literature favors industry experience over general managerial experience.[4] Experience in a startup is said to be especially valuable, but the evidence is largely anecdotal.[5] Venture capitalists appear to value such experience, but its absence is not a major barrier to their support.

The academic literature yields conflicting opinions as to the prevalence

Table 4–2
Variables and Categories Comprised by the New Venture Performance Framework

The Entrepreneur	*The Industry*
Entrepreneurial experience	*Structure of the industry*
Successful	Pure monopoly
Unsuccessful	Homogeneous oligopoly
None	Differentiated oligopoly
	Pure competition
	Monopolistic competition
Managerial experience in a related industry	*Stage of industry evolution*
Yes (# of years)	Development
None	Growth
	Shakeout
	Maturity
	Saturation
	Decline
Startup experience	*Industry disequilibrium*
Successful	Evident
Unsuccessful	Not evident
None	
Education	*Sector of the economy*
Advanced degree	Wholesale
College degree	Retail
MBA degree	Service
No college degree	Manufacturing
	Extractive
	Financial
New Venture Business Strategies	
Competitive substrategies	*Political substrategies*
Reduce production costs new process economies of scale production/technology improvement	Customer contract
Buy in with low price	Favored purchasing
Offer superior product	Rule changes
Discover segment or niche	
Marketing innovation	*Investment substrategies*
Imitative entry geographic transfer supply shortage market relinquishment	High intensity Medium intensity Low intensity

and value of college education among samples of entrepreneurs.[6] Samples containing many craftsman-type entrepreneurs[7] are less relevant to this book than samples of more ambitious entrepreneurs. Venture capitalists, who consider proposals mainly from the latter type of entrepreneur, report finding very few entrepreneurs who do not have a college education. They rely on the college degree largely for validation of technical competence in scientific or engineering ventures. Research has suggested the importance of education to high-technology ventures.[8]

For our purposes, the entrepreneur was described by three essentially objective, biographical data and two subjective criteria. Using biographical data, the entrepreneurs were classified according to industry managerial experience and entrepreneurial experience. They were classified either as having or lacking each type of experience; for those having it, a count of years was used as data. Entrepreneurs were also classified according to their education (number of years beyond high school).

Classification of both entrepreneurial and startup experience as successful or unsuccessful is less objective, as there is no standard definition of success. The categories of new venture performance developed for this research (and explained below) were adapted to this purpose. Startup experience categories were defined as follows:

> *Successful:* The venture survived at least three years and attained profitability or was sold at a capital gain by the original investors.
>
> *Unsuccessful:* The venture failed; or the venture survived beyond three years but never reached profitability or a profitable sellout under this entrepreneur.

Nonstartup entrepreneurial experience has less universal criteria. It requires having been a firm's president or chief executive officer, or the equivalent, but there is no requirement as to the age of the firm. In order to cover both young and established firms, the categories were defined as follows:

> *Successful:* Under this entrepreneur the company grew substantially or was very profitable, depending on its goals.
>
> *Unsuccessful:* Under this entrepreneur the company fell short of its anticipated growth and/or profitability; or the company failed.

Entrepreneurial experience that included multiple startups or multiple presidencies was considered successful if at least half of the episodes would be classified as successful under these standards.

Structural Characteristics of the Industry

The new conceptual framework describes an industry by incorporating its sector of the economy, its stage of evolution, its structure, and the presence or absence of disequilibrium.

Sector of the Economy. A venture's economic sector has been virtually the only industry datum collected in prior new venture research. The studies of mortality rates that Vesper[9] used for intersector comparisons have been, for all their limitations, the new venture academic literature's main contribution. Since venture capitalists express sector preferences, this framework includes the venture's sector of the economy. (The sectors are listed in table 4–2 but are not defined here because none of this study's propositions concerned them.)

Industry Evolution. In chapter 2 venture capitalists were found to consider an industry's stage of evolution, preferring entry into pre-maturity industries. In chapter 3 the concept of industry evolution was shown to have become established as a key element in theory and research in strategic management. Both the choice and the effectiveness of competitive strategies are affected by the industry's stage of evolution.[10] Abell conceptually linked entry strategy directly to industry evolution.[11] Thus the incorporation of industry evolution in this portion of the conceptual framework receives both practitioner and academic support.

I used six stages of industry evolution,[12] described as follows:

Development: Primary demand just beginning, with annual growth still below 15 percent and little evidence of market segmentation. Great changes in product design still occurring.

Growth: Market is growing at least 15 percent per year, and at an increasing rate. Some market segmentation is evident. Changes in product design are great, while process design changes begin. Increasing number of competitors.

Shakeout: While still high, market growth rate has begun a rapid decline. Product design changes less rapidly but process design changes more rapidly than during Growth. Competitors begin dropping out in significant numbers.

Maturity: Market growth approximates rate of increase of the gross national product. Numerous segments may develop. Product design is stable but process design continues to change. The number of competitors stabilizes.

Saturation: Similar to maturity, but the market grows less rapidly than the gross national product and process design stabilizes.

Decline: The market shrinks over several years, and segmentation may diminish. Product design and process design changes are slight. Weaker competitors exit.

Industry Structure. Industry structure is a complex factor. Broad classifications are available as well as considerable theory and research on the effects of individual structural variables. As a first step, each industry is identified as a pure monopoly, homogeneous oligopoly, differentiated oligopoly, pure competition, or monopolistic competition.

The classification of industry structure is based on the industry's degree of product *homogeneity* or *differentiation* and on the number of sellers.[13] Homogeneity and differentiation are opposite attributes of products. Homogeneity suggests perfect substitutibility of rival products; differentiation suggests differences that cause buyers to prefer one firm's product over another's at the same price. These differences may be objectively measurable or purely subjective, image differences.

Pure monopoly exists whenever there is but one seller. The demarcation between *oligopoly* and *competition* is essentially subjective; it depends on whether the sellers are conscious rivals.

The attractiveness of an industry depends on whether it promises above-normal profitability persisting over time.[14] Above-normal profits result from disequilibrium and may be sustained by barriers to entry. Thus both disequilibrium and entry barriers play vital roles in determining industry attractiveness.

Disequilibrium. Disequilibrium exists when more than one price is found in a market for economically equivalent items, especially when a set of resources is valued at less than the price the market pays for what the resources can produce. Disequilibrium is most effectively revealed by successful entrepreneurship.[15] Because such evidence is not available to the prospective entrepreneur, I use "evident disequilibrium" and seek evidence available at the venture's inception.

Disequilibrium is said to arise from rapid industry growth, recent exit of incumbents, high industry rates of capacity utilization, and recent technological changes.[16] Only two of these four conditions could be captured in my research. Growth is embodied in the concept of industry evolution, described above. Exit by incumbents is included because it seemed readily verifiable, at least for major incumbents. (It is also one of Vesper's entry wedges.[17]) However, data on capacity utilization would be unavailable for many subject industries, and interindustry comparisons of technological change were too problematic to be attempted in this book.

Evidence of disequilibrium was sought in contemporary published reports on the industry. It was also sought in the venture business plan.

Barrier to Entry. Above-normal profits are not the sole criterion of industry attractiveness. If many firms should enter the industry, its above-normal profits would prove short-lived. For the above-normal profits born of disequilibrium to persist, entry must be thwarted or never attempted. Entry is deterred by structural barriers and by would-be entrants' fear of retaliation by incumbents. My research draws on Porter's formulation of both sources of deterrents.[18] Structural barriers include the following:

Economies of Scale: A relatively large volume of output is required to attain competitive unit costs.

Product differentiation: Brand identification and/or customer loyalties have been created through earlier dealings, advertising, services, or exposure.

Capital requirements: Up-front costs for facilities, working capital, start-up, and other early needs.

Switching costs: One-time costs facing the buyer who switches from one supplier to another.

Access to distribution channels: Price breaks, cooperative advertising allowances, or other expenses may be necessary to gain access to distributors; or the entrant may be forced to establish entirely new channels.

Cost disadvantages independent of scale: Incumbents' advantages due to proprietary technology, favorable sites or access to raw materials, government subsidies, and the effects of cumulative experience.

Retaliation by incumbents is more likely in industries that possess certain characteristics.[19] The more readily verifiable of these include slow growth, homogeneous products, high fixed costs relative to variable costs, and high industry concentration.

A successful entrant is best positioned to reap above-normal returns when entry barriers increase after entry, thereby securing the entrant's profitability against later arrivals. Barriers may increase either as a result of actions by incumbents or independently of any such actions. A firm is more likely to enter an industry with above-normal profitability if it expects barriers to increase independently or if it believes that it and/or other incumbents will be able to raise the barriers themselves.

An industry is more attractive for entry, then, if disequilibrium exists and the prospect exists for subsequent increases in its barriers to entry.

Venture Business Strategy

Business strategies are expected to affect the performance of new ventures, just as they have been found to affect the performance of established firms.[20] This book's framework incorporates venture business strategy through a synthesis of previous classifications and descriptions introduced in chapter 3.

This strategy construct adheres to the generally accepted concept of strategy consisting of four components:[21] the firm's scope, its distinctive competences resulting from resource deployments, the competitive advantages that result from the firm's combination of scope and resource decisions, and the synergy created by the effects of the first three components as they cut across market and organizational boundaries. Just as these components are combined in certain prevalent patterns to form generic business strategies, they also are the essential parts of new venture business strategies.

The conceptual threads of scope and resource deployment are woven throughout the schemes for classifying new venture business strategies. Hofer and Schendel suggest thinking of business strategy as having three parts, or substrategies: investment, competitive position, and political.[22] At the business level, the investment substrategy describes the level or intensity of resources to be used. The competitive position substrategy tells how those resources will be deployed to advantage. The political substrategy concerns alliances or coalitions that are intended to advance the business's aims. For our purposes, the scope and resource deployment decisions are captured under the headings of competitive substrategy, political substrategy, and investment intensity (as shown in table 4–2).

Competitive Substrategies. The competitive and political substrategies represent a combination of the classification schemes developed by Vesper[23] and Porter.[24] Most of Porter's entry strategies, and some of Vesper's, are competitive substrategies. Most of Vesper's "other entry wedges" are political substrategies. Some changes have been made in combining the Porter and Vesper schemes in table 4–2. To account for what Vesper called "parallel competition" there is an additional competitive substrategy, "imitative entry", that includes geographic transfer, the exploitation of supply shortages, market relinquishment, and positioning as a second source. In each of these instances a new venture is emulating existing firms but relying on differences in scope or resource deployment to secure its future.

Several of Vesper's entry wedges have been dropped in developing this framework. Franchising is excluded because this research deals with independent new ventures with strategic decision-making autonomy. Franchise holders frequently implement plans and techniques that they purchase from the franchisor along with trademarks, formulas, raw materials, equipment, and so on. Although there are exceptions, most franchise holders would not fit the definition of the entrepreneur developed in chapter 3.

Other of Vesper's wedges are not available to independent new ventures. Thus the framework does not include joint ventures, licensing, or the acquisition of corporate divisions as going concerns.

The six competitive substrategies are described as follows:

Reduce product costs: Finding a way to produce at lower costs than incumbents through new process technology, economies of scale, and/or production or technology improvements brought about through more modern facilities.

Buy in with a low price: Gaining market share at the expense of current profitability. (This is not identical to establishing a permanently lower price on the basis of reduced product costs. It is a temporary measure, undertaken with the intention of recouping losses in a later period.)

Offer a superior product: Overcome existing product differentiation with a product innovation.

Discover a segment or niche: Cater to the distinctive requirements of a subset of the market in order to overcome barriers of product differentiation or distribution channels.

Marketing innovation: Overcome product differentiation or the power of distributors through an innovation in marketing.

Imitative entry: Emulate existing firms, relying on the new venture's unique scope or resource deployments. Examples might include *geographic transfer* of a proven concept to virgin territory, exploitation of a *supply shortage* that favors even the undistinguished possessor of the resource or good that is in short supply, or filling the void created through an incumbent's *market relinquishment.*

Business definitions. The description of venture business strategies is completed by the classification of their business definitions. The categories come directly from Abell,[25] who defined the focused, differentiated, and undifferentiated categories in terms of three measures: (1) scope; (2) differentiation of a company's offerings, one from another, across market segments; and (3) differentiation of a company's offerings from those of competitors. Both scope and differentiation are viewed in terms of customer groups served, customer functions performed, and technologies used.

Abell's three alternative types of business definition are described as follows:

Focused: A company has a narrow scope, comprising one or a few segments. It relies on a careful tailoring of its offerings to the needs of those segments. Segmentation may be based on customer groups served, customer functions performed, or the technology used.

Differentiated: A company combines differentiation across any of the three dimensions listed above with a broad scope that places it in numerous segments. The company's offerings differ from segment to segment according to each segment's particular needs. Such differentiation may be coupled with a unique combination of segments (the *scope* measure) to create *competitive differentiation,* which sets a company as a whole apart from its competitors.

Undifferentiated: A company combines broad scope across any or all of the three dimensions with an undifferentiated approach to the segments. This means that the same offerings are made available without tailoring to different customer groups, customer functions, or technology preferences.

These definitions provide a logic to guide the competitive substrategies listed in table 4–2. Table 4–3 indicates the apparent consistency of each competitive substrategy with the three types of business definition. Although not all competitive substrategies lend themselves to use with each business definition, some are suitable for at least two of them. When this is the case, the competitive substrategy may be better understood as a part of the superordinate strategy described by each business definition. For example, the "buy in with low price" competitive substrategy would be constituted and implemented differently by two firms, the one seeking high-volume market dominance through an undifferentiated business definition and the other pursuing a focused business definition and using the temporarily low price to overcome buyers' switching costs.

Political Substrategies. A political substrategy is intended to develop alliances, coalitions, or other forms of external support for a venture. Many variations may exist. The types included in this book are chosen from Vesper's entry wedges:[26]

Customer contract: An advance commitment from a major customer that the venture can use as evidence of viability in pursuing financing, trade credit, other customers, and so forth.

Favored purchasing: An entitlement under certain government programs to preferential treatment in competing for government contracts or business.

Table 4–3
Suitability of Competitive Substrategies to Abell's Business Definition Strategies

	Business Definition Strategies		
Competitive Substrategies	*Undifferentiated*	*Differentiated*	*Focused*
Reduce production costs			
New process	X		
Economies of scale	X X	X	
Production/technology improvements	X		
Buy in with a low price	X	X	X
Offer superior product		X	X
Discover segment or niche		X	X X
Marketing innovation		X X	X
Imitative entry			
Geographic transfer		X	X
Supply shortage	X	X	X
Market relinquishment		perhaps	X

Source: Derek F. Abell, *Defining the Business: The Starting Point of Strategic Planning* (Englewood Cliffs, N.J.: Prentice-Hall, 1980).

Note: X X = Competitive substrategy is highly suitable to business definition strategy; X = competitive substrategy is suitable to business definition strategy.

Rule changes: A change in law or regulations that brings changes in the conditions for entry, basis of competition, or permissible activities within an industry or market.

Venture Performance

The new framework's dependent variable is new venture performance. Performance is largely the result of the influences and interactions of the three factors just discussed. Measurement and evaluation of performance itself, however, is an unresolved issue in organizational research.

This framework adopts as its evaluation criteria the degree of goal attainment by the new venture. Several potential snares are eliminated by the special circumstances of the new ventures whose performance is to be evaluated. First, there is no substantial separation of ownership from management in new ventures. Therefore the question of whose goals to pursue is moot. Second, the decision to exclude small, "mom 'n pop" enterprises substantially reduces the importance of nonfinancial imperatives in the goal sets of sample ventures. The framework is intended to apply to ambitious ventures and their entrepreneurs. It is safe to assume that among this group the desire for independence at mere wage-substitute returns is not the driving force in the entrepreneurial act. Instead, the venture's goals probably include financial return as the foremost objective, whether to be enjoyed in the present or in the form of subsequent capital gains.

Despite the avoidance of some common snares, the measurement of performance does present special difficulties in a diverse sample of new ventures. Because of the diversity of represented industries, for example, the ventures' market shares, activity ratios, and rates of return on sales or assets may not be comparable. The rate of sales growth varies tremendously even among successful new ventures, but differences often owe to this measure's reliance on first-year sales figures. Since new ventures often show meaninglessly low sales during the first year or more of operation, a firm with almost no sales in its first year "outperforms" another firm with modest first-year sales even if the latter is several times larger after both firms have operated for a few years. The short time span of interest in evaluating new venture performance makes impractical any recourse to substituting averages of the first several years as the base figure in sales growth measures.

In light of the uniqueness of a new venture's situation, its performance will be measured categorically. A venture is considered highly successful, successful, marginal, unsuccessful, or highly unsuccessful, depending on which of the statements in table 4–4 best describes its performance. The performance dimensions weighed most heavily in this classification scheme are survival as an enterprise, investors' returns, and profitability.

The measurement of survival is fairly straightforward, and should be understood to include as survivors those enterprises that have changed managers or in which equity interests have been transferred voluntarily. Investors' returns are not so clearcut, since no public market exists for the stock of most new ventures. Instead, investors' returns will be measured by the returns on equity disposed of by venture capitalists or other first-round investors.

In the absence of equity transactions or a highly reliable estimate of market value, performance can be judged on the basis of the venture's profitability. Ventures that are not profitable are not considered successful; among the profitable ventures, the compound rate of return on equity is measured over the venture's history.

Integration of Factors to Form the New Framework

The framework comprises the independent effects of the entrepreneur's characteristics, the industry, and the venture business strategy. Prior research and theory lead me to believe that each of these will play a significant part in determining new venture performance. The model also incorporates joint effects or interaction among these factors, although these effects have received little or no attention in new venture research.

Table 4–4
Categories of New Venture Performance

Venture Category	*Code*	*Venture Performance*
Highly successful	(+ +)	The venture has attained profitability and equity holders have reaped returns of at least 30% per annum[a] when disposing of shares. If no equity has been sold, then ROE has exceeded 30% over the venture's life.
Successful	(+)	The venture has attained profitability but equity holders have not been so well rewarded as in the highly successful venture.
Marginal	(0)	The venture remains alive but is essentially a breakeven operation, or the original equity interests have been replaced, with no gain accruing to them.
Unsuccessful	(−)	The venture still has significant losses or has undergone bankruptcy reorganization.
Highly unsuccessful	(− −)	The venture is defunct because of commercial failure.

[a]This is an industry rule-of-thumb for the desired rate of return on a portfolio of venture capital investments. For a recent indication that this rate remains typical, see Gail Gregg, "Investing in Entrepreneurs," *Venture* (June 1984):46–50.

Macroeconomic variables that could affect new venture performance will not be formally examined in this book. They are omitted from the conceptual framework, although general economic conditions are said to be important considerations in strategy formulation.[27] They may affect new venture performance, although the relationship between prosperity and new venture performance is ill-defined. The difficulty can be traced in part to the same measurement problems that confuse the question of new venture mortality rates,[28] and in part to the difference between new ventures and established small businesses. Thus the known association between economic recessions and higher business failure rates is countered by the increase in the number of ventures begun during recessions. The Austrian theory of the business cycle points out that a depression brings on an unusually large liquidation of malinvestment and a resultant reallocation of resources. New venture formation depends on the reallocation of resources, and new venture performance depends in part on disequilibrium. Both should be more prevalent during recession or depression than during times of stability or prosperity.

Investment intensity is another variable not examined in this book despite its inclusion in the conceptual framework. Adequate data on investment intensity were not available through the chosen research method. The venture business plans did not provide the industry data that would be required in order to measure intensity relative to industry norms. Without such a measure there could be no comparisons between ventures in diverse industries.

Nor was it possible to know the actual investment data for ventures that may have been funded by other sources after approaching the venture capitalists who participated in my research. It is important to realize that the business plans were submitted in order to raise capital and that the size and structuring of the investment were key items to be negotiated. Thus even a detailed business plan can only propose a level of funding.

Research Questions

The seven research questions posed here are intended to probe the several components and relationships of the synthesized framework of new venture performance. These questions share the framework's bases in theory and research.

The first three research questions each involve only one influence on performance. Later questions involve interactions between influences.

(Q1) Which new venture business strategies are more effective than others?

This question lies at the heart of the revised framework and of this research. The strategic management literature provides both theoretical and empirical support for a strategy–performance relationship in established firms. In the development of the revised framework, it was reasoned that new ventures were a special instance of industry entry and that theories or descriptions of entry strategies[29] might usefully be related to those dealing specifically with new ventures. Parallel reasoning leads to the conclusion that business strategies, like entry strategies, affect the performance of new ventures as well as of established firms. In other words, the strategies of new ventures are viewed as a special instance of business strategies, susceptible to the same environmental and competitive forces.

(Q2) How do industry structural characteristics affect new venture performance?

Industry structure enters the framework in much the same way as strategy—by virtue of its role in other models and research, rather than the new venture literature. As was explained in chapter 3, strategic management research increasingly has incorporated dimensions of industry structure previously explored by industrial organization economists. The application of theory and research from industrial organization to new venture performance is justified by reasoning similar to that underlying question 1. Since theory and research have linked industry structure and performance among established firms, and since new ventures can be considered a special instance of general theory in this area, industry structure must affect new venture performance. Further justification can be found in the effects of structural characteristics on entry and intraindustry mobility,[30] since new ventures already have been viewed here as a special instance of entry.

> (Q3) How is new venture performance affected by the characteristics of the entrepreneur?

Entrepreneurship research has addressed this question more regularly than the first and second questions, but without substantially greater success. As was indicated in chapter 3, few research studies have examined entrepreneurial performance rather than propensity, and even fewer have compared successful and unsuccessful entrepreneurs. The strongest evidence suggests that "experience" is important, but it is less clear whether or when entrepreneurial, startup, and industry managerial experience is the most important type. Evidence on the importance of various personality or psychological traits is far from conclusive.[31]

> (Q4) How does the effectiveness of new venture business strategies depend on industry structural characteristics?

This question is the new venture counterpart of the increasingly important strategy–industry structure–performance research in strategic management. The relevance of that research to the new venture is clear, since any industry entrant must overcome, circumvent, or dismantle the various barriers impeding entry. Relying again on the new venture's status as a special instance of the general case, one finds further support for the research's relevance in the importance of industry evolution[32] and structural variables[33] in the choice and effectiveness of entry strategies.

> (Q5) How do the characteristics of the entrepreneur affect the effectiveness of new venture business strategies?

The entrepreneurship literature provides evidence of an association between entrepreneurial type and two venture types that contain elements of strategy.[34] Because the venture types and entrepreneurial types generally represented only two of the four combinations of venture and entrepreneur possible in that study, no conclusions can be drawn as to the relative effectiveness of the two types of entrepreneur in executing either type of strategy.

The strategic management literature recently has begun examining the match between manager and strategy. Reviews of that literature have demonstrated the absence of empirical support for the limited theory developed to date.[35] Many academics and business journalists nevertheless assert the importance of the strategy–manager match on the basis of their own experience and seasoned observation.

(Q6) Are different types of entrepreneur better suited to different types of industry?

Smith's two types of ventures differed in strategies, as noted above.[36] They also differed in several elements of their environments, including volatility of product line and customer mix, geographic breadth of market, and the existence of concrete plans for growth. Thus Smith's Craftsman–Entrepreneur was associated with a relatively stable environment and planned no great changes, whereas the Opportunistic-Entrepreneur operated in a more dynamic environment and planned further changes. To some extent the variables frequently used to assess environmental turbulence, hostility, and complexity are elements or reflections of industry structure. Customers, competitors, suppliers, and government are major factors in models of environmental uncertainty as well as in industrial organization. It is likely that certain types of industries are more hospitable than others to the stability-seeking, less-planned strategy that characterizes Smith's Rigid firm and its Craftsman-Entrepreneur. These industry types may be identifiable by structural characteristics.

(Q7) Are there combinations of venture business strategy, industry structure, and entrepreneur characteristics that bring better new venture performance?

This question is the logical culmination of the other six questions. It represents that combination of all three factors that has been found to be lacking in previous research.

Propositions

The propositions tested were developed from the theory, research, and venture capitalist wisdom described in previous chapters. There is no claim of exhaustiveness in the coverage of these propositions. Instead, this research concentrates on the areas that seem both promising and manageable within the limits of current knowledge and the case-based methodology used. These issues are discussed in chapter 5.

The 19 propositions are grouped to correspond with the order of the research questions. The first 7 propositions deal with venture business strategy.

Strategy Propositions

Distinctive competences and differentiation are at the heart of the strategy propositions. Although there are a multitude of different competences that various business units may develop, the state of theory in the new venture field is not yet adequate to permit the examination of differences between specific competences. Therefore these propositions focus instead on the value of having *any* distinctive competence versus having none. As theory evolves, issues concerning specific competences should become ripe for research.

The importance of distinctive competences has been stressed in both business policy–strategic management and new venture literature, as well as by the venture capitalists interviewed for chapter 2. The theme of distinctive competence reappears in the sources of the venture business strategy classifications used in the framework developed in this chapter.[37]

It is clear in the literature that an effective strategy is based in part on distinctive competence. It is expected that new venture performance will reflect the importance of distinctive competence. Thus a strategy that relies on no particular competence, depending instead on mere imitation of incumbent firms, offers a reduced prospect for success. Entry with a new product or service probably represents some distinctive competence and should outperform imitative entry.[38]

P1: Strategies involving new products or services are more successful than imitative entry.

When the potential advantages of market relinquishment and geographic transfer to virgin territory are removed from imitative entry, only supply shortage remains. This strategy would appear unusually vulnerable in the absence of some factor (such as a politically protected line to a chronically undersupplied resource or an advantageous position with respect to an enforced disequilibrium) to protect the venture from subsequent entry or from retaliation by incumbents. Hence, almost any nonimitative venture business strategy can be presumed to be based on a perceived distinctive competence and can therefore be expected to be superior to a shortage strategy.

P2: Shortage strategies are less successful than nonimitative strategies.

The distinctive competence has a parallel in differentiation from competitors, through which a firm distinguishes itself not by the uniqueness of its product or service but by its unique combination of otherwise unexceptional product or segment positions.[39] This form of differentiation reflects a scope decision, but may be buttressed by the development of competences that are tailored for the unique scope. By differentiating in this manner, a venture can both sidestep entry barriers and reduce the likelihood of effective retaliation by incumbents.[40] With or without such buttressing, a new venture ought to find a strategy of differentiation more consistent with its limited resources than a strategy of industrywide or undifferentiated competition.[41] Although distinctive competences require the commitment of resources, a new venture is expected to be better able to afford and to create the competences demanded by one or a few market segments than the competences—such as low-cost production through scale economies—necessary for industrywide dominance. Furthermore, a new venture's prospects are expected to improve as its scope is defined more narrowly, although a point may be reached where greater narrowness sacrifices potential gains from competing in adjacent, highly similar segments. Hence, there is cause to doubt the relative merits of focusing on very few segments versus differentiating across a somewhat larger number of segments.

P3: Focus strategies are more successful than either industrywide differentiation or cost leadership (using Porter's terminology).

P4: Focused strategies are more successful than undifferentiated strategies (using Abell's terminology).

P5: Focused strategies are more successful than differentiated strategies (using Abell's terminology).

P6: Differentiated strategies are more successful than undifferentiated strategies (using Abell's terminology).

Finally, notwithstanding the difficulty of developing multiple distinctive competences or a broad scope, it is expected that ventures will be more successful when they supplement their primary strategy with a second, complementary strategy.[42]

P7: Venture performance is superior when two or more competitive strategies are used in concert.

Industry Structure Propositions

New venture performance also depends on industry structure variables. The effects of numerous structural variables on entry and performance have been investigated. The literature review and framework presented here have emphasized that product homogeneity discourages entry and encourages strategic retaliation by incumbents.[43] This effect is consistent with the expected superiority of differentiated to undifferentiated strategies, which was stated in proposition 6. Differentiated entry strategies often rely on the heterogeneity of products and competitive strategies found in an industry.[44]

P8: New ventures are less successful in industries with homogeneous products than in those with heterogeneous or partially differentiated products.

An industry's stage of evolution has been identified as an important influence on strategy and performance. Porter extended the analysis to decisions to enter industries.[45] He concluded that entry is more attractive and more feasible when industries are relatively new (since entry barriers have yet to reach later heights) or are growing rapidly (since incumbents will feel less disposed to retaliate while occupied with rapid growth). Both conditions are more likely to obtain in early stages of industry evolution than in later stages.

P9: New ventures are more successful in industries that are in the development or growth stages of evolution.

Because entrepreneurial action is taken on the basis of expectations that depart from the norm,[46] its success depends on the accuracy of the entrepreneur's view of the future. In other words, has the entrepreneur correctly identified and acted upon a disequilibrium, or has the market correctly anticipated and discounted the future? From the concept of the market as an equilibrating process comes a focus on disequilibrium and the factors that perpetuate it. Successful entrants remain successful longer if subsequent entry can be deterred and disequilibrium thereby prolonged.[47]

P10 (a) The presence of disequilibrium makes successful entry more likely.
(b) This effect is more pronounced when disequilibrium is created or sustained by regulatory intervention in the market process, unless to bar entry in the first place.

P11: New venture success is greater when entrants benefit from barriers to subsequent entry.

Entrepreneur's Characteristics Propositions

The entrepreneur's ability to detect opportunities and to exploit them may result in part from innate differences between entrepreneurs and the general populace, but certain types of experience seem to improve his or her chances. In particular, an entrepreneur's performance appears to be enhanced by previous entrepreneurial experience[48] and by managerial experience in a related line of business.[49]

P12: (a) New venture success is more likely when entrepreneurs have prior entrepreneurial experience.

(b) This effect is particularly true when the experience includes a startup venture.

P13: New venture success is more likely when entrepreneurs have prior managerial experience in a related business.

Strategy–Industry Structure Propositions

The effects of industry structure on the strategy–performance relationship and of strategy on the industry structure–performance relationship are expected to be significant. Although ease of entry depends on structural conditions, a venture's exposure to the problems and risks posed by each structural factor will depend on the venture's business strategy. Competitive advantage may be sought through product–market segment positions, distinctive competences, or both.[50] Structural factors that bar successful entry via one segment or distinctive competence may prove ineffective against an alternate entry route. Similarly, opportunities afforded by structural conditions may be exploitable only through certain business strategies.[51]

For example, a new venture that was undifferentiated with respect to segments would find entry difficult in an industry characterized by product differentiation. It would need to develop an advantage that would serve well in numerous segments, since it had chosen not to tailor its offerings to particular segments. A low-cost strategy might create such an advantage, but frequently requires large capital investment and the early achievement of scale economies. A new venture would find these difficult to attain in most established industries.

It has been argued above from an internal, resource-based perspective (as reflected in propositions 3 through 6) that narrower focus or more thorough differentiation improve a venture's prospects. It has also been argued that product homogeneity raises an industry's barriers to entry (proposition 8). The arguments are mutually reinforcing: The best entry strategies rely on a narrowed scope, whereas the most easily entered industries already have at least partial differentiation. The logical foundation of both arguments is the same: New ventures fare better when they can fill an unsatisfied need in an identifiable type of customer, and existing differentiation indicates the potential for further differentiation, since it demonstrates that customers already have differing needs or preferences. Near-commodity status, on the other hand, signifies that no one has discovered a basis for differentiation. (Whether such a basis is nonexistent or merely undiscovered is unknown to us; the first firm to discover it, of course, could be in the best position of all competitors.)

P14: The advantage of differentiated versus undifferentiated strategies is greater when an industry's products are heterogeneous rather than homogeneous.

P15: An undifferentiated strategy is more successful when an industry's products are homogeneous rather than heterogeneous.

Entry by a venture lacking distinctive competence or a novel segmentation scheme has been described as a shortage strategy. Proposition 2 asserted that shortage strategies are inferior to nonimitative strategies in the absence of disequilibrium or political advantage. The success of a shortage strategy evidently depends on the presence of disequilibrium and on the market's ability to reward the successful entrant during the move toward equilibrium.

P16: A shortage strategy is more successful in industries in which disequilibrium is evident.

Another structural influence on the strategy–performance relationship is thought to be the industry's stage of evolution. Abell was specific as to its effects on entry strategy.[52] Each part of the following proposition is based on the conclusions he drew from his field studies. They are adapted from Abell's discussion of entry to the narrower topic of new ventures.

P17: The effectiveness of each type of venture business strategy depends on the stage of evolution of the industry being entered. Specifically:
(a) Differentiated strategies will be more effective in early rather than later stages of evolution.
(b) Undifferentiated strategies will be more effective in early rather than in later stages of evolution.
(c) Broadly defined strategies (that is, differentiated or undifferentiated) will be more effective in early rather than in later stages of evolution.
(d) Focused strategies will be more successful in later rather than in early stages of evolution.
(e) Differentiated strategies will be more successful than focused strategies in early stages of evolution.
(f) Undifferentiated strategies will be more effective than focused strategies in early stages of evolution.
(g) Broadly defined strategies will be more effective than focused strategies in early stages of evolution.
(h) Focused strategies will be more successful than broadly defined strategies in later stages of evolution.

Strategy–Entrepreneur's Characteristics Propositions

The competitive requirements imposed on a new venture extend to the entrepreneur and vary according to the strategy being pursued. Propositions 12 and 13 stated the value of entrepreneurial experience and of experience in a related business. Whereas both forms of experience are expected to be universally valuable, or at worst harmless, their relative importance could be affected by the venture business strategy.

An imitative strategy is based on replication of existing enterprises and practices. A shortage strategy is based on sheer imitation at a propitious moment, and even in geographic extension the entrepreneur can copy firms in other regions. In both imitative and purely shortage strategies, then, replication of existing firms is thought to be sufficient to exploit market opportunities. The skills demanded of entrepreneurs pursuing these strategies may be less general than in other new ventures, where prototypes may not exist. Imitative strategies demand performance of management routines appropriate for the industry entered, and would seem to benefit most from industry-related experience.

P18: Industry experience is more valuable in pursuing an imitative strategy than otherwise.

P19: Entrepreneurial experience is more useful than industry experience in pursuing a nonimitative strategy.

Summary

This chapter began with a comparison of the conceptual frameworks of entrepreneurship and new venture performance that I developed to approximate those in use among academics and venture capitalists. The venture capitalists were found to incorporate more factors, to rely more on subjective and qualitative measurements, and to focus more narrowly—and pragmatically—on venture performance than do the academics, who have developed classification schemes and articulated important strategic concepts more clearly than the practitioners.

A revised conceptual framework of new venture performance was developed through synthesis of the academic and practitioner frameworks. Combining the academics' classification schemes and strategic concepts with the practitioners' richness and performance orientation, the new framework departs from previous academic efforts in its inclusion of venture business strategy and industry structure. This departure is bold enough to constitute a new paradigm of new venture performance.

Following an elaboration of the revised framework, the chapter closes with a presentation of 7 research questions and 19 propositions drawn from theory and research. These propositions are tested, using the research methodology described in chapter 5.

Notes

1. See these works by Robert H. Brockhaus: "Psychological and Environmental Factors Which Distinguish the Successful from the Unsuccessful Entrepreneur: A Longitudinal Study," *Proceedings, Academy of Management,* 1980, pp. 368–372; "Psychology of the Entrepreneur," paper presented at the Conference on Research and Education in Entrepreneurship, St. Louis University, March 1980; "Risk-Taking Propensity of Entrepreneurs," *Academy of Management Journal* 23 (1980):509–520.

2. For example, William M. Hoad and Peter Rosko, *Management Factors Contributing to the Success and Failure of New Small Manufacturers* (Ann Arbor, Mich.: Bureau of Business Research, University of Michigan, 1964).

3. Karl H. Vesper, *New Venture Strategies* (Englewood Cliffs, N.J.: Prentice-Hall, 1980); Arnold C. Cooper, "Strategic Management: New Ventures and Small Business," in *Strategic Management,* edited by Dan E. Schendel and Charles W. Hofer, (Boston: Little, Brown, 1979), pp. 316–327.

4. Robert Buchele, *Business Policy in Growing Firms* (Scranton, Pa.: Chandler Publishing Company, 1967); Hoad and Rosko, *Success and Failure.*

5. Orvis F. Collins and David G. Moore, *The Enterprising Man* (East Lansing, Mich.: Michigan State University, 1964); Lawrence M. Lamont, "What Entrepreneurs Learn from Experience," *Journal of Small Business Management* 10 (July 1972):36–41; Vesper, *New Venture Strategies.*

6. Collins and Moore, *Enterprising Man;* Arnold C. Cooper and William C. Dunkelberg, "Influences Upon Entrepreneurship—A Large-Scale Study," paper presented to the Academy of Management, San Diego, August 1981; Carl M. Larson and Ronald C. Clute, "The Failure Syndrome," *American Journal of Small Business* 4 (October 1974):35–43.

7. Hoad and Rosko, *Success and Failure;* Norman Raymond Smith, *The Entrepreneur and His Firm: The Relationship Between Type of Man and Type of Company* (East Lansing, Mich.: Graduate School of Business Administration, Michigan State University, 1967).

8. Arnold C. Cooper, *The Founding of Technology-based Firms* (Milwaukee Wis.: The Center for Venture Management, 1971); Edward B. Roberts, "A Basic Study of Innovators; How to Keep and Capitalize on Their Talents," *Research Management* 11 (1968):249–266.

9. Vesper, *New Venture Strategies.*

10. Carl R. Anderson and Carl P. Zeithaml, "Stage of the Product Life Cycle, Business Strategy, and Business Performance," *Academy of Management Journal* 27 (1984):5–24; Charles W. Hofer, "Toward a Contingency Theory of Business Strategy," *Academy of Management Journal* 18 (1975):784–810; Charles W. Hofer and Dan E. Schendel, *Strategy Formulation: Analytical Concepts* (St. Paul, Minn.: West

Publishing Co., 1978); Michael E. Porter, *Competitive Strategy* (New York: Free Press, 1980).

11. Derek F. Abell, *Defining the Business: The Starting Point of Strategic Planning* (Englewood Cliffs, N.J.: Prentice-Hall, 1980).

12. This six-stage cycle is based on Hofer and Schendel's approach in *Strategy Formulation*. The PIMS data base uses only four stages: Introduction, Growth, Maturity, and Decline. Hofer and Schendel essentially split Growth (into Growth and Shakeout) and Maturity (into Maturity and Saturation).

13. Definitions of the economic terms can be found in F. M. Scherer, *Industrial Market Structure and Economic Performance* (Chicago: Rand McNally, 1970).

14. Porter, *Competitive Strategy.*

15. Israel M. Kirzner, *Perception, Opportunity, and Profit* (Chicago: University of Chicago Press, 1979).

16. George S. Yip, *Barriers to Entry: A Corporate-Strategy Perspective* (Lexington, Mass.: Lexington Books, 1982).

17. Vesper, *New Venture Strategies.*

18. Porter, *Competitive Strategy.*

19. Ibid.

20. Richard E. Caves and Thomas A. Pugel, *Intraindustry Differences in Conduct and Performance: Viable Strategies in U.S. Manufacturing Industries.* Monograph Series in Finance and Economics (New York: New York University, 1980); Kathryn Rudie Harrigan, *Strategies for Declining Businesses* (Lexington, Mass.: Lexington Books, 1980); Kathryn Rudie Harrigan, *Strategies for Vertical Integration* (Lexington, Mass.: Lexington Books, 1983); Hofer, "Toward a Contingency Theory"; William R. Soukup, "Strategic Responses to Technological Threats," Ph.D. diss., West Lafayette, Ind.: Purdue University, 1979; Carolyn Y. Y. Woo, "Strategies for Low Market Share Businesses," Ph.D. diss., West Lafayette, Ind.: Purdue University, 1980.

21. Hofer and Schendel, *Strategy Formulation.*

22. Ibid.

23. Vesper, *New Venture Strategies.*

24. Porter, *Competitive Strategy.*

25. Abell, *Defining the Business.*

26. Vesper, *New Venture Strategies.*

27. Hofer and Schendel, *Strategy Formulation.*

28. Albert Shapero, "Numbers That Lie," *Inc.* 3 (May 1981): 16–18.

29. For example, Abell, *Defining the Business;* E. Ralph Biggadike, *Corporate Diversification: Entry, Strategy, and Performance* (Boston: Graduate School of Business Administration, Harvard University, 1979); Porter, *Competitive Strategy;* Yip, *Barriers to Entry.*

30. Porter, *Competitive Strategy;* Yip, *Barriers to Entry.*

31. Brockhaus, "Psychology of the Entrepreneur."

32. Abell, *Defining the Business.*

33. Yip, *Barriers to Entry.*

34. Smith, *The Entrepreneur and His Firm.*

35. Anil K. Gupta, "Contingency Linkages Between Strategy and General Manager Characteristics: A Conceptual Examination," *Academy of Management Review*

9 (1984):399–412; Andrew D. Szilagyi and David M. Schweiger, "Matching Managers to Strategies: A Review and Suggested Framework," *Academy of Management Review* 9 (1984):626–637.

36. Smith, *The Entrepreneur and His Firm.*

37. Abell, *Defining the Business;* Porter, *Competitive Strategy;* Vesper, *New Venture Strategies.*

38. Vesper, *New Venture Strategies.*

39. Abell, *Defining the Business.*

40. Yip, *Barriers to Entry.*

41. Buchele, *Business Policy in Growing Firms,* restated in the terminology of Porter.

42. Vesper, *New Venture Strategies.*

43. Porter, *Competitive Strategy;* Yip, *Barriers to Entry.*

44. Yip, *Barriers to Entry.*

45. Porter, *Competitive Strategy.*

46. Ludwig von Mises, *Human Action,* 3rd rev. ed. (Chicago: Henry Regnery Company, 1966).

47. Porter, *Competitive Strategy.*

48. Collins and Moore, *Enterprising Man;* Lamont, "What Entrepreneurs Learn"; Vesper, *New Venture Strategies.*

49. Hoad and Rosko, *Success and Failure.*

50. Hofer and Schendel, *Strategy Formulation.*

51. Yip, *Barriers to Entry.*

52. Abell, *Defining the Business.*

5
Research Design and Methodology

The primary purpose of this book is to contribute to the building of a prescriptive theory of new venture performance that draws on theory and research on venture business strategy, industry structure, and the characteristics of entrepreneurs. Each of these topics has been investigated in other research, but little has been learned of their individual or joint effects on new venture performance. Although the conceptual framework developed in chapter 4 does relate these areas to venture performance, it stops far short of the point at which hypotheses could be tested.

Concept-development and *hypothesis-generation* types of research are prerequisites to hypothesis testing. These types respectively draw and refine *maps of the territory* being studied.[1] Only after hypotheses are carefully developed can hypothesis-testing research be undertaken. My research straddles the concept-development and hypothesis-generation types. It was necessary to map some of the territory, exploring the identity of key variables and the relationships among them.

The review of research in strategic management and industrial organization has established the futility of pursuing universal prescriptive theory involving these areas. Considering the diversity of types and influences encompassed by new venture strategy, industry structure, and the entrepreneur's characteristics, only a contingency theory offers the hope of valid prescriptions for new ventures.

Contingency theories can be constructed by combining corroborated limited-domain theories. (The latter are theories that apply to organizations of a particular type and/or under particular circumstances.) Because the areas of new venture strategy and industry structure generally lack prescriptive theory, it is not yet possible to combine corroborated limited-domain theories to build a theory of new venture performance. Instead, territories must be mapped and integrated prior to testing propositions. The new conceptual framework undertook these tasks and led to a series of propositions about new venture performance. The remainder of this book involves the gathering and analyzing of the data used to test these propositions. These theory-building steps required an appropriate methodology.

Research Design

The unit of analysis in this book is the individual venture. Any broader focus would fail to capture the importance of the venture's business strategy and the entrepreneur's characteristics. I compare longitudinal case studies of new ventures, as Schendel and Hofer suggested doing in exploratory and concept development research.[2]

Research in business policy and strategic management has evolved in two streams: case studies and data base surveys. Case studies capture nuances and details of strategy, competition, and environmental forces, but do so at the expense of generalizability. Data base surveys attain generalizability and statistical significance but sacrifice the knowledge of interacting forces within each observation. Harrigan suggested a hybrid, "medium-grained" methodology in which generalizability and rich detail coexist through the use of large samples of case studies.[3] She noted that most medium-grained research has been exploratory and that, as a consequence, "few studies have exploited opportunities to impose greater rigor on their analyses by incorporating testable hypotheses in their sample designs."[4]

A medium-grained research methodology was used in order to enhance the generalizability of its findings while retaining some of the desirable characteristics of case studies. The decision to develop and use longitudinal case studies was crucial to studying the effects and interactions of strategic variables at the firm level. But while Schendel and Hofer suggested "few" or "several" "focused comparative longitudinal case studies" in research designed for concept development or hypothesis generation,[5] this research used substantially more cases in order to permit statistical analysis. Considerations of time and expense ultimately limited the sample to 17 ventures—far fewer than in data base studies but enough to permit statistical tests.

As will be described below, the sample was selected to provide coverage of the venture categories of interest. As Harrigan recommended, the sample was gathered "using a design which categorizes target firms according to important explanatory variables,"[6] in this instance based on strategy and industry structure.

Selection of Sample

Ventures were drawn from among new venture proposals submitted to four separate venture capitalists between 1974 and 1982. The offices of the venture capitalists were in New York, Atlanta, and Houston. They included two whom I interviewed at length in preparing chapter 2, the private venture capitalist and the investment banker described in that chapter. The third contributor of venture data was a private venture capital investor whose function was quite similar to that of the private venture capital firm, but who also earned consulting income. The fourth participant was a member of a large venture capital firm that sometimes ranked among the 100 largest in the United States. Since he provided access to his firm's files, the sample ventures represent the experience of several venture capitalists within his firm.

The participating venture capitalists provided the following numbers of ventures: the private firm, two ventures; the private investor, two ventures; the investment banker, six ventures; the large venture capital firm, seven ventures. As a condition of their participation in this research, the venture capitalists and their firms were promised anonymity and were guaranteed that there would be no second-guessing of their investment decisions. Therefore the ventures will not be identified with specific venture capitalists, nor will the performances of venture capitalists be compared.

The two participants who had not been interviewed nevertheless talked at length about their views and practices in evaluating new ventures. All four venture capitalist participants appeared to be representative of their industry.

The 17 ventures were chosen to represent the combinations of strategy–industry structure–entrepreneur that were of greatest interest in testing my propositions. Each venture capitalist provided his entire file of venture proposals received between 1974 and 1982. (Although some maintained complete files of all proposals received, others had not retained every proposal. Some had been discarded almost immediately because they seemed hopelessly unattractive, and others were discarded years later during periodic cleanups. Whether through design or inertia, however, nearly all of the venture capitalists with whom I talked during my research had retained some proposals for ventures in which they did not invest and that may never have been launched.)

I classified the ventures according to the categories of strategy, industry structure, and entrepreneur that were described in chapter 4 and listed in table 4–2. I also screened the sample to ensure that all were indeed new or recent startups and that all fell within classifications of interest to this research. It should be emphasized that I used only the venture proposals in classifying and screening the ventures; performance data remained unknown to me at this stage of the research.

Data and Data-Gathering Method

The problem of inaccurate and biased data in retrospective reports is a potentially serious limitation in strategic management research.[7] Therefore, the most sensitive classification data were extracted from the venture proposals, business plans, offering memoranda, and other contemporary documents still in the possession of the participating venture capitalists. Assignment to strategy categories was based solely on prestartup documents in order to avoid post hoc rationalizations on the part of entrepreneurs and venture capitalists alike. Industry structure data sometimes were obtained from industry experts or published sources, including some that were written after the venture's startup. (In no case did these sources include the entrepreneur, venture capitalist, or others associated with the venture.)

Following the classification of the independent variables, venture performance data were obtained from the venture capitalists and from public sources. Among the annual data sought were sales, net income, cash flow, return on equity, and market share. In the event that the venture capitalist was unable or unwilling to provide this information, the researcher asked the venture capitalist to assign the venture to the proper performance category in table 4–4. Three venture capitalists provided relatively complete performance data, while one provided none. No significant venture performance difference was found on the basis of whether performance data were provided.

Tests were also conducted for other effects in the sample. Since the ventures were founded in different years, the possibility of macroeconomic effects was considered. The ventures were placed in three roughly equal cohorts, consisting of the five ventures begun in 1974–1977, the seven begun in 1978–1979, and the five begun in 1980–1981. The most significant difference was the advantage of the 1980–1981 group over the 1978–1979 group ($.172 < p < .216$ on the Mann–Whitney U test). Venture age effects also were examined, and venture performance was unrelated to the number of years of data on the venture (Spearman $r = .024$, $p > .45$ on a one-tailed test).

Appendix A is the form used to record the relevant information on each venture. It provides a detailed description of the data sought.

Classification Methods

The process for classifying each entrepreneur, venture business strategy, and industry consisted of four steps: (1) defining the categories for each factor; (2) my classification of each venture's entrepreneur, business strategy, and industry; (3) an independent expert's classification of the business strategy; and (4) the reconciliation of any differences between (2) and (3).

The definitions used for classification are presented in the following sections. They follow as closely as possible the definitions used in the literature reviewed in chapter 3. Consistency in repeated applications by me and in replications by others is more likely if generally recognized, accepted, and understood definitions are used. Departures from this principle were taken only when consensus definitions were lacking or were incomplete for the purposes of my research.

The independent expert whose judgment served to corroborate the strategy classifications was a member of the graduate faculty in business policy at a research-oriented university. He was thoroughly familiar with the relevant sections of the Abell and Porter books[8] and was provided with written descriptions of the business definition categories and with the descriptions of each venture's business strategy that appear in appendix B. (Note that the expert was given no performance data.)

The expert's independent classification of the business definitions (that is, differentiated, undifferentiated, or focused) matched mine in 13 of the 17 ventures for a 76.5 percent initial agreement on the three-way classification. The null hypothesis of randomness in agreement (that is, that the expert and I would agree one-third of the time) was rejected ($p < .001$). Through detailed discussion, these differences were resolved and final agreement reached.[9]

Analysis of Data

In selecting techniques for data analysis, a researcher must consider the nature of the populations under study and the limitations of the available data. It is desirable, of course, to use a powerful statistical test, meaning one that has a high probability of rejecting a false null hypothesis. However, the most powerful tests are those that have the strongest or most extensive assumptions about the population and data to which they are applied. Parametric tests are the most powerful and should be used when the necessary conditions are met. For the t test, these assumed conditions include (1) independence of observations; (2) normal populations; (3) homoscedasticity (equal variances) of populations; and (4) the measurement of variables on an interval scale, permitting arithmetic operations on the data.[10]

The populations and data in this book violate at least one of the four assumptions and are suspect in the case of two others. The performance measures are ordinal rather than interval, which clearly violates the fourth condition. In fact, Siegel emphasizes that "parametric statistical tests . . . ought not to be used with data in an ordinal scale."[11] (The ordinal scale was chosen in order to broaden the available sample and to keep the data-gathering tasks manageable.)

The assumption of normal distributions within the populations would be a doubtful one in this instance. Little is known about the survival rate among new ventures or about the distribution of their performances. There is little justification for assuming normal distributions in the various subpopulations defined by the industry structure and strategy categories used in this book, as no empirical research exists to provide even a suggestion of the statistical properties of these subpopulations.

The subpopulation variances are subject to the same lack of empirical research, but the assumption of homoscedasticity is subject to a more serious objection as well. There are theoretical grounds to *expect* variances to differ between the subpopulations being compared. Certain firm-specific differences in strategies or industry structure are believed to cause different levels of firm-specific financial risk.[12] In other words, one expects to find different variances in financial returns between subpopulations defined by strategies or industry structures. These are precisely the bases for classifying ventures in this research.

Because parametric statistical tests are inappropriate to ordinal scales and because the population does not meet other assumptions of parametric tests, nonparametric statistical tests were used. Siegel[13] discusses the assumptions made by nonparametric tests. The acceptability of these assumptions in the case of this study is demonstrated elsewhere.[14]

Each of the propositions stated in chapter 4 involves comparisons of two independent populations through measurements made on an ordinal scale. The sample classifications are usually nominal. Several nonparametric statistical tests suit the requirements of this general case. Because differences in central tendency (rather than differences in dispersion, skewness, or other respects) are of primary interest in the propositions being examined, either the Mann–Whitney *U* test or the Kolmogorov–Smirnov one-tailed test is appropriate. Although the Kolmogorov–Smirnov test is somewhat more efficient for very small samples, the Mann–Whitney *U* test was chosen for its ability to discriminate between populations with relatively small differences in central tendency but markedly different frequency distributions in the high-end and low-end performance categories.[15]

Certain propositions involve the measurement of correlation between an entrepreneur's previous experience, expressed in years, and venture performance. The Spearman rank correlation coefficient was chosen for these tests because its computation does not depend on the forced ranking of entrepreneurs who were tied in years of experience. While random ordering would resolve ties, the large proportion of ties (especially at zero years of experience) in a sample of 17 raised too great a threat of spurious correlations if the Kendall tau were used. The small sample also prevented the use of regression models.

The selection of nonparametric statistics imposes some limitations on this research. Most notable is the inability of the chosen tests to measure the magnitude (as distinguished from the significance) of statistical relationships. This is important in two ways. First, one lacks a measure of a factor's bottom-line impact on performance. Since many of the factors (for example, differentiation, new products, or low-cost positions) are created only through the commitment of a venture's resources, a measure of magnitude would permit a useful comparison of the benefits and costs of creating them.

Second, it is more difficult to compare the effects of two different factors. Both effects may be statistically significant, yet one factor could be pivotal in determining the fates of new ventures, whereas the other could be of only minor importance despite its statistical significance.

Other limitations of this research ought to be kept in mind when interpreting its data and conclusions. These limitations as well as the statistical limitations are discussed in chapter 6.

Summary

This chapter began by recalling the purpose of this research, which is to develop theory and prepare for the testing of hypotheses that would explain new venture performance in terms of factors that have proved fruitful in strategic management and industrial organization economics research. The design of this research was likened to the "medium-grained" research that Harrigan has espoused for similar purposes.

The source of the data and the methods by which they were gathered were discussed. Appendix A provides more details on the data that were sought. The classification procedures were described, including the role of an independent expert in the classification of business definitions.

Finally the chapter discussed the statistical methods and tests to be used in analyzing the data. Nonparametric statistics were chosen due to their greater suitability to the nature of the data and the size of the sample. Specifically, the Mann-Whitney *U* test and the Spearman rank correlation statistic were selected for this purpose.

Notes

1. Dan E. Schendel and Charles W. Hofer, ed., *Strategic Management* (Boston: Little, Brown, 1979), p. 387.
2. Ibid.
3. Kathryn Rudie Harrigan, "Research Methodologies for Contingency Approaches to Business Strategy," *Academy of Management Review* 8 (1983):398–405.
4. Ibid., p. 400.
5. Schendel and Hofer, *Strategic Management,* p. 387.
6. Harrigan, "Research methodologies," p. 400.
7. Daniel J. Power and George P. Huber, "Guidelines for Using Key Informants and Retrospective Reports in Strategic Management Research," in *Proceedings of the 14th Annual Meeting of the American Institute of Decision Sciences,* pp. 29–31.
8. Derek F. Abell, *Defining the Business: The Starting Point for Strategic Plan-*

ning (Englewood Cliffs, N. J.: Prentice-Hall, 1980); Michael E. Porter, *Competitive Strategy* (New York: Free Press, 1980).

9. My dissertation provides greater detail on the expert's qualifications and on the process by which we resolved classification differences. See William R. Sandberg, "The Determinants of New Venture Performance: Strategy, Industry Structure and Entrepreneur," Ph.D. diss., Athens, Ga.: University of Georgia, 1984.

10. The conditions assumed by parametric tests are described in Sidney Siegel, *Nonparametric Statistics for the Behavioral Sciences* (New York: McGraw-Hill, 1956).

11. Ibid., p. 26.

12. Richard A. Bettis, "Modern Financial Theory, Corporate Strategy, and Public Policy: Three Conundrums," *Academy of Management Review* 8 (1983): 406–415.

13. Siegel, *Nonparametric Statistics.*

14. Sandberg, "Determinants of New Venture Performance."

15. Siegel, *Nonparametric Statistics.*

6
Results and Analysis

This chapter presents and analyzes the data on the performance effects of venture business strategies, industry structure, and the characteristics of the entrepreneur. These effects are examined first individually, and then in combination. The format is consistent: Under each major heading (for example, Industry Structure), each proposition is restated, followed by the data and their statistical interpretation.

Following the data presentation, I discuss the results as a whole. My intention is to interpret the results and relate them to other research and to the conceptual framework developed in chapter 4. In particular, I will argue that both strategy and industry structure affect new venture performance and that their respective effects are not independent of each other. Several possibilities are discussed. At the broadest level of abstraction on both strategic and structural dimensions, the data suggest a contingent relationship in which early-stage entrants prosper with broadly defined strategies (either differentiated or undifferentiated) and later-stage entrants are more successful when pursuing focused strategies.

The chapter concludes with a discussion of the limitations inherent in this research. There are certain qualifications that should be borne in mind when interpreting the results, and cautions that should be heeded in receiving the conclusions.

Results and Analysis

The sample is described in table 6–1, which provides category totals for the new venture performance framework. Each venture's strategy is summarized in appendix B. Table 6–2 shows the venture strategy and industry structure data used in testing the propositions. (Data on the entrepreneurs are found in table 6–13.)

Table 6–1
Number of Ventures in Each Category of the New Venture Performance Framework

The Entrepreneur	*The Industry*
Entrepreneurial experience	*Structure of the industry*
(7) successful	(0) pure monopoly
(1) unsuccessful	(1) homogeneous oligopoly
(9) none	(2) differentiated oligopoly
	(7) pure competition
	(7) monopolistic competition
Managerial experience in a related industry	*Stage of industry evolution*
(11) yes	(1) development
(6) no	(10) growth
	(1) shakeout
	(5) maturity
	(0) saturation
	(0) decline
Startup experience	*Industry disequilibrium*
(7) successful	(5) evident
(1) unsuccessful	(12) not evident
(9) none	
Education	*Sector of the economy*
(3) advanced degree	(0) wholesale
(8) college degree	(2) retail
(2) M.B.A. degree	(9) service
(1) no college degree	(4) manufacturing
(3) data missing	(2) extractive
	(0) financial

New Venture Business Strategies

Competitive substrategies	*Political substrategies*
Reduce production costs	(2) Customer contract
(1) new process	
(0) economies of scale	
(0) production/technology improvement	
(1) Buy in with low price	(0) Favored purchasing
(4) Offer superior product	(0) Rule changes
(5) Discover segment or niche	
(2) Marketing innovation	

Table 6–1 continued

New Venture Business Strategies
Imitative entry
(1) geographic transfer
(7) supply shortage
(1) market relinquishment

Effectiveness of Business Strategies

Seven propositions were developed from the discussion of the importance of the business strategies chosen by new ventures.

(P1) Strategies involving new products or services are more successful than imitative entry.

Only two ventures used new products or services, whereas eight relied on imitative entry as defined by Vesper.[1] The data in table 6–3 show that new product or service strategies did outperform imitative-entry strategies but that the difference was not significant.

(P2) Shortage strategies are less successful than nonimitative strategies.

The value of possessing distinctive competences led to the belief that strategies presumably based on some sort of distinctive competence would outperform shortage strategies, which require no distinctive competence or differentiation from competitors. (One venture pursued a geographic transfer imitative strategy and thus was not included in either group.) As is shown in table 6–4, the seven ventures pursuing shortage strategies did not perform as well as the nine nonimitative ventures. The result is not considered significant ($p < .20$).

The following proposition concerns the relative effectiveness of venture business strategies classified according to Porter's typology.[2]

(P3) Focus strategies are more successful than either industrywide differentiation or cost leadership.

The results were contrary to the expected direction in both cases under proposition 3, so much so that the data in table 6–5 indicate a significant ($p < .075$) advantage of industrywide differentiation relative to focus strategies. Differentiation was also superior to cost leadership, but only at $p = .190$. Cost leadership and focus were essentially tied, with equal mean

Table 6–2
Summary of Venture Business Strategies and Industry Structures

			Nonimitative		*Imitative*		*Porter's Strategy Classification*		
Venture	*Performance*	*Business Description*[a]	*New Product*	*Other*	*Shortage*	*Other*	*Differentiated*	*Cost-based*	*Focus*
A	+ +	Oil & Gas Drilling			X			[b]	
B	+	Drilling & Workover			X			X	
C	+	Oilfield Services			X			X	
D	– –	Coal Mining			X			[b]	
E	–	Coal Mining			X			[b]	
F	0	RR Freight Car Leas'g			X				X
G	+	Integrated Circuits		X			X		
H	+ +	Medical Svc & Equpmt	X				X		
I	+	Process Control Syst		X			X		
J	0	CADD Software	X						X
K	+ +	Xmas Tree Decor		X					X
L	+	Computer Stores		X			X		
M	+	Electronic Games		X			X		
N	– –	Computer Services			X			[b]	
O	0	Auto Parts Stores		X					X
P	–	Ceiling Fan Mfr		X				X	
Q	– –	Airline				X			X

Sources: Michael E. Porter, *Competitive Strategy: Techniques for Analyzing Industries and Competitors* (New York: Free Press, 1980); Derek F. Abell, *Defining the Business: The Starting Point of Strategic Planning* (Englewood Cliffs, N.J.: Prentice-Hall, 1980).

Note: + + = Highly successful; + = successful; 0 = marginal; – = unsuccessful; – – = highly unsuccessful. These terms are defined in Table 4–4.

[a]Refer to Appendix B for detailed descriptions of the ventures' businesses and strategies.

[b]Industrywide, undifferentiated strategy without a low-cost position.

ranks and central tendencies. The two industrywide strategies combined outperformed focus strategies ($.101 < p < .134$).

Following these results, the possibility was considered that breadth of scope made the difference in proposition 3. An additional test was conducted in which the five ventures lacking both differentiation and cost leadership strategies, but having an industrywide scope, were compared to the five focus strategy ventures. The latter performed better, but the difference was not significant ($p > .345$).

Abell's Strategy Classification			*Multiple Competitive Substrategies Used?*	*Industry's Product Classification*			*Industry's Stage of Evolution*				*Is Disequilibrium Evident?*	*Barriers to Subsequent Entry?*
Differentiated	*Undifferentiated*	*Focused*		*Homogeneous*	*Partially differentiated*	*Heterogeneous*	*Development*	*Growth*	*Shakeout*	*Maturity*		
	X				X			X			Yes	Yes
	X		Yes		X			X			Yes	Yes
	X				X			X			Yes	Yes
	X			X						X		
	X			X						X		
		X	Yes	X				X			Yes	
X						X		X				Yes
X			Yes			X	X					Yes
X						X		X				
		X				X		X				
		X	Yes		X					X	Yes	
X					X			X				
X						X		X				
	X				X			X				
		X		X						X		
X					X				X			
		X			X					X		

The next three propositions concern the relative effectiveness of Abell's business definition strategies.[3]

(P4) Focused strategies are more successful than undifferentiated strategies.

The five focused strategy ventures did outperform the six undifferentiated ventures, as indicated in table 6–6. This difference was expected but was not considered significant ($p < .409$).

(P5) Focused strategies are more successful than differentiated strategies.

As might be expected following the results of proposition 3, the six ventures with differentiated strategies outperformed the five with focused strat-

Table 6–3
Performance of New Product or Service Strategies and of Imitative Entry Strategies

	Venture Performance					
	+ +	+	*0*	–	– –	*Total*
New product/service	1	0	1	0	0	2
Imitative entry	1	2	1	1	3	8

New product/service > Imitative entry: $U = 4$; $p = .20$.

Table 6–4
Performance of Nonimitative Strategies and Shortage Strategies

	Venture Performance					
	+ +	+	*0*	–	– –	*Total*
Nonimitative	2	4	2	1	0	9
Shortage	1	2	1	1	2	7

Nonimitative > Shortage: $U = 20.5$; $\chi^2 = 3.33$; $p = .20$.
Note: The Kolmogorov-Smirnov test was used because the value of U greatly exceeded the critical values tabled in Sidney Siegel, *Nonparametric Statistics for the Behavioral Sciences* (New York: McGraw-Hill Book Company, 1956) for samples of this size.

egies. The data in table 6–6 show the superiority of the differentiated strategies, which was significant at $p < .165$ when tested as a new proposition.

The reversed versions of propositions 3 and 5 were tested because of the uncertainty, referred to in chapter 4, as to when narrower scope ceases to be an advantage and instead sacrifices profitable, easily captured business in closely related segments. Since this research is designed to build theory, statistical testing of reversed propositions was deemed useful.

(P6) Differentiated strategies are more successful than undifferentiated strategies.

The results in table 6–6 show a difference in the predicted direction but falling short of acceptable statistical significance ($p = .197$).

The pattern that emerges from the first six propositions provides consistent (but often statistically weak) support for the value of differentiation and relatively broad scope. The strongest finding (significant at $p < .075$) was the superiority of Porter's industrywide differentiation to a focus strat-

Table 6–5
Performance of Focus, Industrywide Differentiation, and Cost Leadership Strategies

	Venture Performance					
	+ +	+	*0*	–	– –	*Total*
Focus	1	0	3	0	1	5
Industrywide differentiation	1	4	0	0	0	5
Cost leadership	0	1	0	1	0	2
Broad scope only, strategyless	1	1	0	1	2	5

Industrywide differentiation > Focus: $U = 4.5$; $.048 < p < .075$.
Focus > Cost leadership: $U = 5$; $p = .571$.
Industrywide differentiation > Cost leadership: $U = 2$; $p = .190$.
Focus > Broad scope only, strategyless: $U = 10.5$; $p < .421$.

Table 6–6
Performance of Differentiated, Focused and Undifferentiated Strategies

	Venture Performance					
	+ +	+	*0*	–	– –	*Total*
Differentiated	1	4	0	1	0	6
Focused	1	0	3	0	1	5
Undifferentiated	1	2	0	1	2	6

Differentiated > Focused: $U = 8.5$; $.123 < p < .165$.
Differentiated > Undifferentiated: $U = 12$; $p = .197$.
Focused > Undifferentiated: $U = 15.5$; $p < .409$.

egy; the same tendency was suggested ($p < .165$) when Abell's classification was used to examine differentiated and focused strategies. The expected advantage of the more narrowly targeted strategies was not evident; in fact the more broadly defined strategies were stronger performers.

The final strategy proposition asserts the value of multiple competitive strategies used in concert.

(P7) Venture performance is superior when two or more competitive strategies are used in concert.

Only 4 ventures used a second competitive strategy. Their performance was superior to the 13 other ventures, as indicated in table 6–7. The difference was in the predicted direction but was not significant.

Table 6–7
Performance of Ventures Using Multiple Competitive Strategies

	Venture Performance					
	+ +	+	*0*	–	– –	*Total*
Multiple competitive strategies	2	1	1	0	0	4
All other ventures	1	5	2	2	3	13

Multiple competitive strategies > All other ventures: $U = 11.5$; $\hat{p} = .221$.
Note: Because U exceeded the tabled critical values, the statistic $\hat{p}$ was used as an unbiased estimator of p ($\hat{p} = U/N_1N_2$). Source: Leonard A. Marascuilo and Maryellen McSweeney, *Nonparametric and Distribution-Free Methods for the Social Sciences* (Monterey, Calif.: Brooks/Cole Publishing Company, 1977), page 272.

Industry Structure

Three propositions concerned the effect of industry structure on new venture performance.

(P8) New ventures are less successful in industries with homogeneous products than in those with (a) heterogeneous or (b) partially differentiated products.

There were four ventures in industries with homogeneous products, eight in industries with partially differentiated products, and five in industries with heterogeneous products. The data in table 6–8 show the superior performance of entries in the heterogeneous and partially differentiated industries relative to those in homogeneous industries. The most significant difference ($p = .016$) favors entry into heterogeneous over homogeneous industries. The advantage of ventures in partially differentiated industries was far less significant ($p < .184$) and approximated that of heterogeneous over partially differentiated industries ($p < .217$).

(P9) New ventures are more successful in industries that are in the development or growth stages of evolution.

Eleven ventures entered industries that were classified as being in the development or growth stages of evolution and 6 entered industries that had passed into shakeout or maturity. As can be seen in table 6–9, 10 of 11 early-stage entrants were highly successful, successful, or marginal. The 6 latter-stage entrants fared poorly by comparison ($p < .05$.)

(P10) (a) The presence of disequilibrium makes successful entry more likely.

Table 6–8
Performance of Ventures in Heterogeneous, Partially Differentiated, and Homogeneous Industries

	Venture Performance					
	+ +	+	*0*	–	– –	*Total*
Heterogeneous industry	1	3	1	0	0	5
Partially differentiated industry	2	3	0	1	2	8
Homogeneous industry	0	0	2	1	1	4

Heterogeneous industry > Homogeneous industry: $U = 1; p = .016$.
Partially differentiated industry > Homogeneous industry: $U = 9.5; .141 < p < .184$.
Heterogeneous industry > Partially differentiated industry: $U = 13.5; .144 < p < .217$.

Table 6–9
Performance of Ventures Grouped According to Industry's Stage of Evolution

	Venture Performance					
	+ +	+	*0*	–	– –	*Total*
Development or growth stages	2	6	2	0	1	11
Shakeout, maturity, or saturation stages	1	0	1	2	2	6

Early stages > Late stages: $U = 15; p < .05$.

(b) This effect is more pronounced when disequilibrium is created or sustained by regulatory intervention in the market process (unless to bar entry).

I used "evident disequilibrium" as my standard rather than risk an after-the-fact equating of disequilibrium with new venture success, as was explained in chapter 5. Evident disequilibrium was said to exist when prestart-up evidence suggested that economically equivalent items brought different market prices or that a complex of resources could be acquired for less than the market price of what the resources could produce.

Five ventures attempted to enter industries characterized by evident disequilibrium, and all succeeded in establishing a position in their industry. Two were classified as successful and two as highly successful.

The fifth venture, in railroad freight car leasing, became a marginal performer with slightly better than breakeven performance in its fourth year, but the cash flows were quite acceptable to its investors even while it had shown a loss. The performance of this venture suffered considerably with the demise of a favorable disequilibrium that had been imposed by regulators. (The venture leased hopper cars, then in short supply, to shippers who found railroads unable to guarantee car availability due to the Interstate Commerce Commission's "equitable service" orders. In addition to this aspect of federal regulation, disequilibrium was evident in the state government's enforcement of higher freight tariffs for railroad-provided cars than for leased ones; this permitted the lessor to add a lease fee to the tariff and still underprice the railroad. The substantial deregulation of railroad rates changed car utilization patterns and pricing practices and removed this venture's built-in advantage of disequilibrium.)

Since the effect of disequilibrium is the object of proposition 10(a), it seemed reasonable to treat the railroad hopper car leasing venture as a successful entry. The venture entered, established a viable market position, and generated an acceptable (to its investors) cash flow while the government induced and maintained a disequilibrium; its performance deteriorated only when the government withdrew its enforcement of the disequilibrium.

The data in table 6–10 show superior performance for ventures entering industries that are in disequilibrium. The difference is significant at $p = .05$. Reassignment of the hopper leasing venture to the successful category yields a difference that is significant at $p < .025$. Only this venture fit the special circumstances of proposition 10(b), so no statistical test was performed and the example's support of 10(b) is considered merely anecdotal.

(P11) New venture success is greater when entrants have the benefits of barriers to subsequent entry.

Five ventures enjoyed barriers to subsequent entry. Three (ventures A, B, and C) benefited from the scarcity of drilling rigs and related capital goods after their entry. The other two erected barriers themselves through patent protection of technology (G and H) and through proprietary joint research activities with customers (H). The data in table 6–11 show that ventures enjoying such barriers to subsequent entry were more successful than other ventures. The performance difference was significant at $p < .025$.

The possibility was considered that ventures benefiting from subsequent input scarcity, and thus from barriers acquired or developed at no cost to the venture, performed better than ventures that erected (and thus may have paid for) barriers themselves. The small sample yielded no significant difference.

Characteristics of the Entrepreneur

The next two propositions concern the value of entrepreneurial experience and related managerial experience.

Table 6–10
Performance of Ventures Grouped According to Presence of Disequilibrium

	Venture Performance					
	+ +	+	*0*	−	− −	*Total*
With Venture F classified as marginal						
Disequilibrium was present	2	2	1	0	0	5
Disequilibrium was not present	1	4	2	2	3	12
With Venture F classified as successful						
Disequilibrium was present	2	3	0	0	0	5
Disequilibrium was not present	1	4	2	2	3	12

Disequilibrium present > Not present:
Venture F classified Marginal: $U = 13$; $p = .05$.
Venture F classified Successful: $U = 10.5$; $p < .025$.

Table 6–11
Performance of Ventures Grouped According to Presence of Barriers to Subsequent Entry

	Venture Performance					
	+ +	+	*0*	−	− −	*Total*
Barriers subsequently arose	2	3	0	0	0	5
No barriers arose	1	3	3	2	3	12

Barriers subsequently arose > No barriers arose: $U = 8.5$; $p < .025$.

(P12) (a) New venture success is more likely when entrepreneurs have prior entrepreneurial experience.
(b) This effect is particularly true when the experience includes a startup venture.

Eight entrepreneurs had prior entrepreneurial experience ranging in duration from 1 to more than 10 years. Contrary to the proposition, the 9 first-time entrepreneurs had superior performance as shown in tables 6–12 and 6–13. Entrepreneurial experience and venture performance had a Spearman rank correlation of $r = -.056$ but the difference did not approach significance ($p < .45$). The second part of this proposition was untestable because all experienced entrepreneurs had startup experience.

(P13) New venture success is more likely when entrepreneurs have prior managerial experience in a related industry.

Table 6–12
Performance of Ventures Grouped According to the Entrepreneur's Prior Entrepreneurial Experience

	Venture Performance					
	+ +	+	0	–	– –	*Total*
Entrepreneurial experience	2	2	0	2	2	8
None	1	4	3	0	1	9

Note: The mean performance of inexperienced entrepreneurs surpassed that of experienced entrepreneurs when the performance categories were converted to a five-point scale. This was contrary to expectations but not significant.

Table 6–13
Performance of Ventures, Characteristics of Entrepreneurs, and Imitativeness of Strategies

		Years of Experience				*Imitative Strategy?*	
Venture	*Performance*	*As Entrepreneur*	*As Manager in Similar Industry*	*Years of College*	*Age*	*Yes*	*No*
A	+ +	0	5	6	32	X	
B	+	0	8	4	33	X	
C	+	0	0	0	50	X	
D	– –	4	4	[a]	[a]	X	
E	–	3	0	6	40	X	
F	0	0	10	6	40	X	
G	+	0	0	8	[a]		X
H	+ +	5	0	6	42		X
I	+	1	4	4	30		X
J	0	0	2	5	28		X
K	+ +	10+	10+	4	47		X
L	+	0	7	[a]	[a]		X
M	+	10+	10	4	42		X
N	– –	0	0	4	38	X	
O	0	0	0	4	32		X
P	–	6	7	4	49		X
Q	– –	10+	10+	[a]	50	X	
Spearman r =		–.056	.077	.14	–.09		

[a]Data unavailable.

Eleven entrepreneurs had prior managerial experience in a related industry. Their ventures displayed better performance than those of the six who lacked such experience but the difference was not significant. As table 6–13 indicates, the Spearman rank correlation was .077 ($p < .40$).

One must be cautious in drawing conclusions from the tests of propositions 12 and 13. Do not infer that either type of experience is of no consequence to an entrepreneur. The conclusion drawn here is merely that neither type of experience explains or is associated with the performance of the ventures in this sample.

The research also examined the relationships between venture performance and the entrepreneur's age and education. Both were tested with the Spearman rank correlation for samples of 14 ventures, as age data were unavailable for one venture, education data for another, and both for two other ventures. Age was negatively associated with venture performance ($r = -.09$), whereas education, measured by years of college, was positively associated ($r = .14$), but neither was significant ($p < .40$).

Correlations were not noticeably stronger when the sample was divided into early-stage and late-stage entries. I had speculated that industry experience might make a difference in mature industries but found no significant correlation ($r = -.06$); the correlation for 11 early-stage entries was essentially identical ($r = -.05$).

It had also seemed plausible that entrepreneurial experience would be especially valuable in early-stage industries. Although its relationship with performance was positive ($r = .35$), it was not quite significant ($p < .15$). Among late-stage entries, the relationship was negative ($r = -.16$) but not significant. Startup experience had no significant effect samplewide and was significant only at $p < .188$ for the early-stage entries.

Multiple Factors

To this point the propositions have considered only one factor at a time. This limitation was relaxed in the remaining propositions. The following three propositions combine venture business strategy and industry structure.

> (P14) The advantage of differentiated versus undifferentiated strategies is greater when an industry's products are heterogeneous.

None of the five ventures in heterogeneous industries used an undifferentiated strategy, and none of the four in homogeneous industries used a differentiated strategy. The resultant empty cells prevented testing of this proposition.

While empty cells are a hazard of small-sample research, the absence of ventures from these two strategy–structure combinations may be significant in a practical (if not statistical) sense. For example, the undifferentiated strategy–heterogeneous industry combination was expected to be ineffective, but proved nonexistent. Avoidance of certain strategies in specific industry settings suggests a practitioner consensus on their inadvisability.

(P15) An undifferentiated strategy is more successful when an industry's products are homogeneous rather than heterogeneous.

The aforementioned absence of undifferentiated strategies among the five ventures in heterogeneous industries also prevented a test of this proposition. Instead homogeneous and partially differentiated industries were compared, with the results shown in table 6–14. Contrary to expectations, the undifferentiated strategies performed better in partially differentiated industries, although the coincidence of two coal mining ventures constituting one set should be weighed against even this weak effect.

(P16) A shortage strategy is more successful in industries in which disequilibrium is evident.

In testing proposition 2 it was found that the seven ventures pursuing shortage strategies did not perform as well as the nine nonimitative ventures. In testing proposition 16, those seven ventures were grouped according to the presence or absence of disequilibrium in their industries. The data in table 6–15 indicate a clear difference in performance. All three ventures entering industries that were in equilibrium were unsuccessful, whereas the four ventures entering industries that were in disequilibrium were successful or, at worst, marginal. (The marginal performance of venture F has been attributed to the removal of regulatory controls that sustained disequilibrium in railroad hopper car leasing.) The performance difference is in the predicted direction and is significant at $p = .028$.

(P17) The effectiveness of each type of venture strategy varies with the stage of evolution of the industry being entered. Specifically,
(a) differentiated strategies will be more effective in early rather than in later stages of evolution;
(b) undifferentiated strategies will be more effective in early rather than in later stages of evolution;
(c) broadly defined strategies (that is, differentiated and undifferentiated) will be more effective in early rather than in later stages of evolution;
(d) focused strategies will be more successful in later rather than in early stages of evolution;

Table 6–14
Performance of Undifferentiated Strategies in Homogeneous and Partially Differentiated Industries

	Venture Performance					
	+ +	+	*0*	–	– –	*Total*
Homogeneous	0	0	0	1	1	2
Partially differentiated	1	2	0	0	1	4

Partially differentiated > Homogeneous: $U = 1.5$; $.133 < p < .276$.

Table 6–15
Effect of Disequilibrium on Performance of Shortage Strategies

	Venture Performance					
	+ +	+	*0*	–	– –	*Total*
Disequilibrium present	1	2	1	0	0	4
No disequilibrium	0	0	0	1	2	3

Disequilibrium present > No disequilibrium: $U = 0$; $p = .028$.

(e) differentiated strategies will be more successful than focused strategies in early stages of evolution;
(f) undifferentiated strategies will be more effective than focused strategies in early stages of evolution;
(g) broadly defined strategies will be more effective than focused strategies in early stages of evolution;
(h) focused strategies will be more successful than broadly defined strategies in later stages of evolution.

(a) Of the six ventures using a differentiated strategy, only the ceiling fan manufacturer entered a mature industry. Its unsuccessful performance was in contrast to the unanimous success of the five ventures that used this strategy in early-stage industries, as shown in table 6–16. The level of significance ($p = .167$) is the greatest attainable for a sample of this size,[4] indicating that the proposition has received the strongest support possible under the circumstances.

(b) Six ventures pursued undifferentiated strategies. As the data in table 6–16 show, four entered early-stage industries and experienced mixed results; three succeeded (one highly) and the fourth was highly unsuccessful. The two late-stage entrants were less fortunate; one underwent bankruptcy reorga-

Table 6–16
Performance of Ventures Grouped According to Strategy and Stage of Industry Evolution

	Venture Performance											
	Early Stages						*Late Stages*					
	+ +	+	*0*	–	– –	*Total*	+ +	+	*0*	–	– –	*Total*
Differentiated strategy	1	4	0	0	0	5	0	0	0	1	0	1
Undifferentiated strategy	1	2	0	0	1	4	0	0	0	1	1	2
Subtotal:												
Broadly defined	2	6	0	0	1	9	0	0	0	2	1	3
Focused strategy	0	0	2	0	0	2	1	0	1	0	1	3
Stage total	2	6	2	0	1	11	1	0	1	2	2	6

(a) Differentiated Strategy, Early > Late: $U = 0$; $p = .167$.
(b) Undifferentiated Strategy, Early > Late: $U = 1.5$; $p < .267$.
(c) Broad Strategies, Early > Late: $U = 2.5$; $p < .05$.
(d) Focused Strategies, Late > Early: $U = 3$; $p = .60$.
(e) Early Stage, Differentiated > Focused: $U = 0$; $p = .047$.
(f) Early Stage, Undifferentiated > Focused: $U = 2$; $p = .267$.
(g) Early Stage, Broad > Focused: $U = 2$; $p = .111$.
(h) Late Stage, Focused > Broad: $U = 2.5$; $p < .350$.

nization and the other failed completely. Although the measured difference in this small sample was in the predicted direction, it was weak ($.133 < p < .267$).

(c) Combining the first two parts of proposition 17, 17(c) compared the performance of the broadly defined strategies (differentiated or undifferentiated) in early and late stages of industry evolution. Table 6–16 shows that the early-stage subsample included two highly successful, six successful, and only one highly unsuccessful venture, whereas all three late-stage entrants were unsuccessful. The difference is in the predicted direction and is significant at $p < .05$. (The possibility was considered that the differentiated strategy alone accounted for the observed between-stage difference. Although there was no proposition concerning differentiated and undifferentiated strategies in early-stage industries, tests showed no significant difference between the two ($p = .452$).

(d) Three ventures pursued focused strategies in the late stage, with the widely varied results shown in table 6–16. Both early-stage, focused-strategy entrants were marginal performers, and the difference between the two groups was not significant.

(e) Among early-stage entrants, the five differentiated strategies produced one highly successful and four successful ventures. Both focused-strategy ventures were marginal. The difference was in the predicted direction and was significant at $p = .047$, as shown in table 6–16.

(f) The performance of the four undifferentiated, early-stage ventures was superior to that of the focused strategies, as expected, but the difference was not significant (see table 6–16).

(g) Combining the samples from (e) and (f), we find the nine broad-definition strategies outperforming the two focused strategies in the early stage ($p < .11$).

(h) In the late stage there were six ventures, evenly divided between broad and focused strategies. While focused strategies outperformed the broadly defined strategies, as expected, the difference was not significant. Breaking the broad strategies into differentiated and undifferentiated groups showed a continued superiority for focused strategies, although significance again was lacking (versus differentiated, $N_1 = 1$, $N_2 = 3$, $p = .500$; versus undifferentiated, $N_1 = 2$, $N_2 = 3$, $p = .300$).

The remaining propositions concern the value of industry experience and entrepreneurial experience in pursuing particular strategies.

> (P18) Industry experience is more valuable in pursuing an imitative strategy than otherwise.

Eight ventures adopted imitative strategies, as indicated in table 6–13. Within this group, performance correlated negatively with years of managerial experience in similar industries ($r = -.37$). Although not significant, this was not in the expected direction. The nine other ventures displayed a positive Spearman rank correlation ($r = .12$) which was not significant, either.

> (P19) Entrepreneurial experience is more useful than industry experience in pursuing a nonimitative strategy.

Nine ventures pursued nonimitative strategies. In testing proposition 18, industry experience and performance were found to be weakly correlated ($r = .12$) among this group. As can be seen in table 6–13, entrepreneurial experience and performance were more strongly correlated ($r = .36$), but the correlation likewise was not significant.

Discussion of Results

Before interpreting and discussing the results of this research, it is worth recalling its purpose and limitations. The propositions tested in this chapter responded to research questions that inquired into how each of three distinct areas of theory (strategy, industry structure, entrepreneur's characteristics) was related to venture performance, then broadened to encompass two or all three areas.

What can and cannot be concluded from the statistical tests to which these data were subjected? The nonparametric tests provide a very close equivalent in some instances to the power of appropriate parametric statistics. There is probably an overall loss of information compared to what could be gotten through parametric tests, but there is also less danger of "adding information" by treating ordinal as interval data and imprudently assuming normal distributions for the various populations being examined. The chosen procedures are conservative. In other words, the tests understate rather than overstate the performance differences between categories of ventures.

The weakness of this approach is its reduced ability to detect differences, and thus its potential for Type II errors (falsely accepting the null hypothesis of no difference). Thus a finding of nonsignificance must be interpreted cautiously. Rather than being accepted as evidence that some variable plays no part in determining new venture performance, it should be taken as evidence that this method, applied to these data, found no significant difference related to that variable.

With these purposes and statistical limitations in mind, we turn to an interpretation of the results. The three areas will be considered separately at first, and then in combination.

Characteristics of the Entrepreneur

Analysis of the data on these 17 ventures brings to the fore an immediate question: What happened to the expected effects of the entrepreneur's characteristics? Proposition 12 and 13 argued for the value of experience, but neither found support stronger than $p < .40$, meaning that entrepreneurial experience and managerial experience in a related line of business were not significantly associated with the performance of these ventures. This finding conflicts with the consensus of researchers, who assign importance to both industry experience[5] and entrepreneurial experience, particularly involving a startup.[6] It should be noted once more that seven of the eight entrepreneurially experienced entrepreneurs had experienced at least one prior startup. Startup experience came closest to statistical significance among the entrants in early-stage industries. Given the near-congruence of the experienced and startup-experienced groups, it is not surprising that entrepreneurial experience also reached its greatest significance in early-stage industries.

The lesser impact of entrepreneurial or startup experience in late-stage industries may signify its lesser value, of course, but could also denote the ability of other factors to compensate for inexperience when entering late-stage industries. For example, when entering a stable industry, intimate knowledge of the recipes for success in that industry may be more important than nonindustry entrepreneurial experience. Although this sample was too small to permit investigation of such possibilities, the effects of managerial experience were considered.

Despite its support in the literature, industry-related managerial experience failed to approach significance. It is possible that entrepreneurs who lacked such experience had hired experienced associates. Venture capitalists often prefer a management team that includes industry experience. Therefore, one might expect to find more of these management teams among this sample, who sought venture capital, than among the new venture population as a whole. A more diverse sample would include more small business owner/operator types, whose lower financial objectives and greater emphasis on personal goals militate against sharing either responsibility or equity interests.[7]

The failure to identify significant effects of the entrepreneur's age and education should be viewed as generally consistent with other research. Age was not expected to make a difference in venture performance but was tested as a precaution against an unexpected effect. Education did not vary much among the entrepreneurs in this sample; of the 14 on whom this information was available, 13 had spent at least four years in college. Thus the absence of a significant effect may indicate the absence of a noticeable difference among the subjects. It is possible, though, that the trend toward more widespread (and, some allege, more badly diluted) college education has reduced its significance in the two decades since the studies by Hoad and Rosko.[8]

Apart from the effects of startup and entrepreneurial experience on early-stage entries, the measured characteristics of the entrepreneur appear not to have played a significant role in the performance of these new ventures. It is possible, of course, that other characteristics, not examined here, do affect venture performance. Venture capitalists certainly place considerable emphasis on their or others' assessments of an entrepreneur's track record, desire, and so forth. Indeed their amalgam of biographical and subjective or impressionistic data may be as valid as any other approach to assessing entrepreneurial aptitude, particularly in light of the very limited success in using psychological variables to predict venture performance.[9]

The two remaining broad areas of inquiry proved more fruitful. Both venture business strategy and industry structure seem to play important roles. They will now be considered, first separately and then in conjunction with each other. Table 6–17 summarizes significant findings.

Venture Business Strategy

Propositions 1 and 2 examined the importance of distinctive competences and scope as components of new venture business strategy. Having distinctive competences, it was reasoned, would enable ventures offering new products

Table 6–17
Significant Findings of Statistical Tests of This Book's Propositions

Proposition	*Finding*	*Significance*
3	Industrywide differentiation strategies outperform focus strategies.	$p < .075$
8	New ventures are more successful in industries with heterogeneous products than those with homogeneous products.	$p = .016$
9	New ventures are more successful in industries that are in the development or growth stages of evolution.	$p < .05$
10	Disequilibrium makes successful entry more likely.	$p = .05$[a]
11	Barriers to subsequent entry lead to greater new venture success.	$p < .025$
16	Shortage strategies are more successful when an industry is in disequilibrium.	$p = .028$
17	Broadly defined strategies are more effective in early than in late stages of industry evolution.	$p < .05$
17	Differentiated strategies outperform focused strategies in early stages of industry evolution.	$p = .047$
17	Broadly defined strategies outperform focused strategies in the early stages of industry evolution.	$\hat{p} = .11$[b]

[a]As was explained in the text, reclassification of one venture's entry performance yields $p < .025$.

[b]$\hat{p}$ is an unbiased estimator of p. Refer to the note to table 6–7.

or services to outperform imitative ventures. Further, it was argued that since nonimitative strategies were built on some distinctive competence or another, whereas shortage strategies were the purest form of imitation, the former should outperform the latter.

Although both arguments were supported, the support was significant only at about $p = .20$. While distinctive competence may be important, its contribution to venture performance appears not to be decisive in and of itself. This may reflect several factors. First, even if it be conceded that all new products or services embody distinctive competences, they may face additional difficulties because of their newness. The costs of gaining access to existing channels of distribution or of winning credibility among potential buyers may offset the advantages of distinctive competences.

Second, the value of distinctive competences ought to be contingent on the nature of the market being entered and specifically on the extent of competition to be encountered there. Since the value of a distinctive competence derives from its utility in setting a firm apart from its competitors in some respect that the market values, it follows that the distinctive competence is most useful in competitive markets and least useful in noncompetitive ones.

A market in disequilibrium is, for at least the present, not highly competitive. Thus a venture that correctly anticipates a market disequilibrium and exploits it with a shortage strategy may have no immediate need for a distinctive competence. The failure to support proposition 2 at better than $p < .20$ may reflect such accurate diagnosis and timely action by some of the entrepreneurs who pursued shortage strategies.

Both of these lines of reasoning suggest the importance of industry structure. Such possibilities will be considered further when structure is discussed later in this chapter.

The generic strategies provided additional significant findings. The results of propositions 3, 4, 5, and 6 as a whole argue for the value of differentiation combined with a broad business definition.

Industrywide differentiation (as in proposition 3) means competing in virtually all segments on the basis of one or more attributes that are "perceived industrywide as being unique."[10] This generic strategy significantly outperformed the narrowly defined focus strategy, which relies on either differentiation or cost leadership that applies only within selected niches or small segments rather than across the entire industry. (Cost-based industrywide strategies offered no improvement over focus strategies in the two-venture sample available here. It is possible, of course, that few ventures attain the sales volume necessary to realize economies of scale.)

These results appear to be consistent with Biggadike's finding that corporate ventures by PIMS participants performed better when they sought volume and attained scale economies than when they focused more narrowly on a small segment or niche.[11] Despite the relatively broad scope adopted by most of his sample, Biggadike suggested that some segmentation had been built into his sample through the somewhat narrowed business definitions used in the PIMS data base. If he is correct on this point, then his findings would support the use of differentiated as well as cost-based industrywide strategies for entrants.

More important in assessing the impact of differentiation is the finding that the five ventures that broadly defined their scopes but lacked distinctive competences and cost leadership did not perform as well as the three focus ventures. Taken with the significant superiority of differentiated over focus strategies, this points to the importance of distinctive competence. Breadth of scope, unaided by distinctive competence, appears to offer new ventures an insufficient basis for competitive advantage.

Concepts similar to Porter's were covered by propositions 4 through 6, which were based on Abell's business definition strategies.[12] Abell defined differentiation differently from Porter. To Abell, a differentiated business definition could be attained through several methods, including the provision of different products across market segments. To Porter, a differentiation strategy meant creating one difference that is recognized industrywide. In this study, only venture P, the manufacturer of ceiling fans, would be classified differently by the Abell and Porter schemes. Venture P sought to have lower production and distribution costs than its competitors, to compete in nearly every price and quality segment, and to offer substantially different fans in different segments. In my judgment the differentiation across segments was intended to be venture P's principal hope for success, and the cost advantage was clearly secondary. In Porter's scheme, though, this would not be considered industrywide differentiation because the venture was not relying on a single difference from rival fans that would be valued across the various segments. Thus for the purposes of proposition 3, which tested Porter's strategies, venture P was classified as using a low-cost industrywide strategy.

It must also be noted that Abell's undifferentiated strategy accomodates both Porter's industrywide low-cost competitor and a firm with broad scope and no distinctive competence or cost advantage. It might be expected, then, that this strategy will fare poorly in comparison to the others, as it absorbs the essentially strategyless ventures that in prior tests failed to perform as well as focus strategy ventures.

Differentiated strategies again performed better than focused strategies, although at a somewhat diminished level of significance ($p < .165$). The change is attributable to the presence in the differentiated strategy sample of venture P, which was unsuccessful. Despite the weakened performance among the differentiated group, it surpassed the undifferentiated ventures, although the difference was not significant ($p = .197$). The direction of difference and level of significance are essentially identical to those found earlier in comparing differentiated and cost leadership strategies ($p = .190$), and further conform to the belief that differentiation is important when a venture seeks broad scope.

The strategy propositions also suggest the value of multiple distinctive competences in the form of secondary competitive substrategies. Some competitive substrategies do not involve distinctive competences. For example, venture K counted on a competitor's market relinquishment to make available some large accounts even while using production improvements to lower their own costs. Other competitive substrategies do yield multiple distinctive competences, though. For example, venture H offered new superior medical testing equipment and innovatively developed competences in sports medicine by working with professional teams to diagnose injuries to players.

The four ventures that used multiple competitive substrategies performed better than the other ventures. Whether through additional distinctive competences or through shrewd scope decisions, these ventures appear to have benefited from enhanced differentiation.

In sum, the sample ventures indicate the value of distinctive competence when coupled with an appropriate choice of scope. The broader scope of a differentiated strategy apparently permitted wider application of distinctive competences than a focused strategy, without sacrificing the venture's distinctiveness. At the same time, the distinctive competences paid off in stronger performance than was attained through the undifferentiated strategies, which lacked distinctive competences other than cost positions.

A broad scope without differentiation, as in the undifferentiated strategy, performed less well than a narrow scope supported by distinctive competences. (No ventures were found to have combined a narrow scope and an undifferentiated approach. The two conditions appear inconsistent, provided that scope is assumed to have a meaningful definition in terms of product–market segments. If a venture is not attempting differentiation, why should it limit itself to a specific niche or segment?)

The levels of significance reported for these data do not permit the confidence one would require of tested theory. Reasonably strong support for the superiority of differentiated over focused strategies does not constitute a non-contingent theory of new venture performance. Whereas the failure to find highly significant support for non-contingent strategic propositions might be attributable to the small sample or to information lost through the design of this research, it is also entirely consistent with research in the business policy or strategic management field.

The desirability of a contingency approach to strategy research was articulated a decade ago by Hofer, and its necessity has since been demonstrated many times.[13] Strategic management research has turned to industry structure as a moderating variable in the strategy–performance relationship. It is to industry structure that this study turned as well.

Industry Structure

An obvious conclusion to be drawn from the data on propositions 8 through 11 is that these new ventures were affected by industry structure much as any other firm, and as other industry entrants in particular. The statistical significance with which these propositions were supported was impressive in two respects. First, the levels of significance were high for a sample of only 17, as three of four propositions were supported at better than $p = .05$. Second, the uniformity of support was striking, as even the weakest support attained $p = .10$.

Quite apart from the impact of any one dimension of industry structure, it is important to appreciate the meaning of the "obvious conclusion" drawn here. If all four distinct propositions received support at significant levels, there is a powerful case to be made for bringing the concepts and tools of industrial organization economics into new venture research. Prior research did not take advantage of them, but there now is evidence that this neglect has reduced the explanatory and predictive capabilities of new venture theory. Implications of these points for researchers will be discussed in chapter 7.

The results are important in their narrower sense, too. The impacts of individual structural variables can be identified and interpreted from these data. The general topic of barriers to entry covers most of the findings, with special attention given to the roles of industry and product homogeneity or heterogeneity.

For the 17 ventures studied, entry was clearly more successful in industries having heterogeneous products. The performance advantage was most clear for heterogeneous versus homogeneous products ($p = .016$), but there was weak support as well for differences between intermediate levels of industry differentiation. In light of the significant difference between the heterogeneous and homogeneous groups, the weaker advantages of heterogeneous over partially differentiated groups ($p < .217$) and of partially differentiated over homogeneous groups ($p < .184$) are mutually consistent and arguably more significant than these conservative tests on small samples have been able to discover.

These findings are consistent with those of Yip. Like his, they are in contrast to the traditional industrial organization economics view that differentiation poses strictly an entry barrier. According to Yip, the structural variables that create barriers may even denote "the existence of gateway effects such that entrants can obtain advantages by virtue of being entrants."[14] More specifically, "structural variables contribute to both the height of barriers and the strategic heterogeneity mitigating them" as incumbents cannot collectively make use of all viable strategies.[15]

Yip's explanation for the seemingly paradoxical effect of entry barriers is supported by the results of the strategy propositions, reported above. Recalling that differentiated strategies were found to outperform undifferentiated strategies, albeit not at a significant level, one can infer that the existence of strategic heterogeneity (and its correlate, product heterogeneity) opens the way for successful differentiation. A differentiated strategy, therefore, would seem especially appropriate in an industry characterized by product heterogeneity. This potential interaction of strategy and industry structure is the subject of the next set of propositions.

Yip also pointed out the role of disequilibrium in mitigating the effects of entry barriers. Short-run factors contributing to disequilibrium included technological change, exit of incumbents, high capacity utilization, and rapid industry growth. Although this study used a more limited definition of disequilibrium that emphasized external impediments to equilibrium (such as unavailability of capital goods or necessary inputs and regulatory intervention that prevented the emergence of a single, market-clearing price), its results nevertheless tend to confirm Yip's view. Evident disequilibrium aided both initial entry ($p < .025$) and longer-term performance ($p = .05$). These findings are conservative to the extent that the definition of disequilibrium omitted factors that aid venture performance and that were included by Yip.

Industry growth rate was the only factor among those omitted here to be found significant by Yip; it is captured to a considerable extent in this book's industry evolution propositions.

New ventures also benefited significantly from subsequent increases in the height of entry barriers ($p < .025$). This is consistent with industrial organization theory, since at some point the new venture becomes an incumbent, seeking to maintain the level of profitability that lured it into the industry in the first place. Whether such barriers are worth erecting at some cost to the venture or are worthwhile only if the benefits are cost-free consequences of some other firm's or party's actions is a question left unanswered by these data.

Ventures appear to be affected by industry evolution, too. Those entering industries in the development or growth stages of evolution significantly outperformed the later-stage entrants ($p < .05$). This may reflect the importance of industry growth rate, which Yip treated as an indicator of possible disequilibrium. It could also result from the fluidity associated with early stages of evolution, when new bases for competition and new methods of operation are still being discovered or developed, and to the shifting of competition to bases (such as production economies, financial strength, and logistical advantages)[16] that are less advantageous to new ventures. Indeed, stages of industry evolution often are explicitly linked to industry structure[17] and have been used as an efficient encapsulation of structural factors (in conceptual form by Hofer and Schendel[18] and in a research application by Anderson and Zeithaml[19]). Industry evolution seems a conceptually appealing and tractable substitute for the complex web of industry structural variables. This possibility has not been lost on strategic management researchers, as noted by Anderson and Zeithaml, and seems equally alluring to a new venture researcher. The possibility was pursued in the final set of propositions.

Venture Business Strategy and Industry Structure

Empty cells prevented testing of two basic propositions concerning the relationship between strategy and industry structure. Thus, no conclusion can be stated about the performance of differentiated and undifferentiated strategies in heterogeneous and homogeneous industries. The effect of industry structure on the strategy–performance relationship was evident, however, in the case of shortage strategies. Despite their generally inferior performance in proposition 2, which was significant at $p < .20$, there was a distinction among shortage strategies. They performed better when industries were in disequilibrium ($p = .028$). Because disequilibrium was defined more narrowly here than elsewhere, some of the shortage-strategy ventures may have been in industries that were not classified as being in disequilibrium but that would have been by other researchers. Thus, some of the advantaged class may have been classified as disadvantaged; even so, a significant difference appeared. (Any classification error of this type would have a conservative effect.)

Greater success came in relating performance to the combination of venture business strategy and stage of industry evolution. Significant performance differences were found among strategies within stages (called a "strategy effect") and between stages for given strategies (called a "stage effect").

The strongest stage effect was observed among broadly defined strategies, where the early-stage entrants were more successful than late-stage entrants ($p < .05$). Both the differentiated and undifferentiated strategies displayed the same stage effect, at roughly the same level of significance ($p = .167$ and $.133 < p < .267$, respectively) within their respective samples of six ventures. No stage effect was detected among the five focused-strategy ventures; indeed one cannot even say which group performed more strongly, since their central tendencies were identical and no clear risk preference can be identified. Without a risk preference it is impossible to weigh the performance of two marginal-performance ventures against that of a group comprising one highly successful, one marginal, and one highly unsuccessful venture.

The detection of a significant stage effect within a strategy group is consistent with strategic management theory and research.[20] Simply stated, a stage effect means that there are better and worse situations in which to use a particular strategy, depending on the stage of evolution of the industry in question. Based on the precedent established in strategic management research and on the results reported here, it seems likely that the effectiveness of venture business strategies is dependent on the stage of evolution of the industry being entered.

The 17 ventures also provide clear evidence of strategy effects within stages. Among early-stage entrants, differentiated strategies were clearly superior to focused strategies ($p = .047$), and the four ventures with undifferentiated strategies outperformed the two with focused strategies (although the difference was not significant). Combined, the broadly defined strategies outperformed the focused strategies ($p = .11$). In the late stages of evolution quite another relationship existed, though. Focused strategies were superior to broadly defined strategies, although significance was lacking in the sample of six ventures.

These strategy and stage effects offer confirmation of propositions that appear not to have been subjected to testing in prior research. Abell recommended using differentiated strategies when entering growth stage markets and focused strategies when entering mature ones.[21] He also recommended either focused or undifferentiated strategies for pioneering entries (that is, the development stage). Two caveats should be kept in mind in extending Abell's recommendations to the present context. First, he was referring to entry

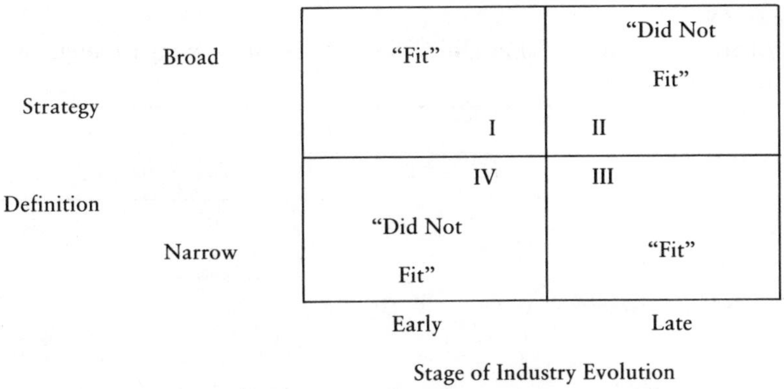

Strategy Definition		Early	Late
	Broad	"Fit" I	"Did Not Fit" II
	Narrow	IV "Did Not Fit"	III "Fit"

Stage of Industry Evolution

Figure 6–1. Successful Combinations of Strategy Definition and Stage of Industry Evolution Are Indicated by "Fit"

rather than to new ventures, so his prescriptions were intended to apply as well to moves by established firms. Second, he reported them as conclusions from his field studies, but performed no statistical tests to confirm their accuracy.

Taken together, Abell's recommendations can be presented as a prescriptive matrix, as in figure 6–1. One dimension classifies industry evolution; the other classifies breadth of strategy definition. Ventures in cells one and three fit the prescriptions of Abell, while those in cells two and four do not. Based on proposition 17(g), broadly defined strategies are better than focused strategies in early stages, so one expects the ventures in cell one to outperform those in cell four. Based on proposition 17(c), broad strategies work better in early than in later stages, so ventures in cell one should outperform those in cell two. Both expectations received significant statistical support. Focused strategies are expected to be more effective than broadly defined strategies among late-stage entrants (proposition 17[h], with only weak support) and focused strategies should perform better among late-stage than early-stage entrants (proposition 17[d], no difference detected). Thus, cell three likewise would be expected to outperform its vertical and horizontal neighbors. Although not all between-cell comparisons received strong support, none was reversed.

On the basis of proposition 17, then, one would expect ventures that fit (those in cells one and three) to outperform the ventures that do not fit (those in cells two and four). In strategy–stage terms, both Broad–Early and Focused–Late are appropriate, whereas any other combination of strategy and stage is not.

Twelve ventures followed the prescriptions of proposition 17 while five

Table 6–18
Performance of Ventures That Did and Did Not Fit Strategy to Stage of Industry Evolution

	Venture Performance					
	+ +	+	*0*	−	− −	*Total*
Strategy/stage fit	3	6	1	0	2	12
Strategy/stage did not fit	0	0	2	2	1	5

Strategy/stage fit > Strategy/stage did not fit: $U = 10$; $p < .025$.

did not. Table 6–18 compares the performance of these two sets. Among the twelve "fits" were *all three* highly successful, *all six* successful, one marginal, and two highly unsuccessful ventures. The five ventures that did not follow the prescriptions included *no* successful or highly successful ventures. The difference in performance was significant at $p < .025$, establishing the superior performance of ventures that fit the contingent prescriptions.

A pronounced difference appears between the two cells that do *not* match strategy and industry evolution. When the two Focused–Early ventures are compared to the three Broad–Late ventures, their performance is better ($U = 0$, $p = .10$). This finding is consistent with the belief that focused strategies in early-stage industries are undesirable largely because they fail to take advantage of all opportunities, whereas broad strategies in late-stage industries are undesirable because they produce so many failures. The five ventures in the two "non-fit" cells show precisely this performance pattern.

The importance of these findings is twofold. First, they reiterate the evidence on the key portions of proposition 17 that assert both stage and strategy effects on venture performance.

More important, they provide a theoretically coherent, cohesive basis for addressing the various effects of venture business strategy and industry evolution. In earlier chapters the argument was made on behalf of a new conceptual framework of new venture performance, $NVP = f(E, IS, S)$. The results of my research provide important corroboration of the roles played by industry structure and venture business strategy in determining the performance of new ventures. The failure to find significant performance effects associated with the characteristics of entrepreneurs may reflect the nature of the data and tests used. On the other hand, prior research has not established such effects either.

Instead of $NVP = f(E)$, the conceptual framework that has predominated in academic thinking about new venture performance, the results of my research support the new framework proposed in earlier chapters. Certainly a framework of new venture performance ought to incorporate industry structure and new venture business strategy. To avoid prematurely excluding the characteristics of the entrepreneur, pending further research, the framework ought to retain this factor. To reflect its weak support both in prior research and in this study, however, this factor will be relegated to a position of less prominence in the functional expression of the new framework. In discussing the implications of this study for venture capitalists, entrepreneurs, and researchers, I shall now write the conceptual framework of new venture performance as $NVP = f(IS, S, E)$.

Limitations of This Research

The interpretation and use of the data and findings of this research remain subject to several limitations. There are three major sources of such limitations. The first comprises the research design and the conceptual framework, which omitted certain factors from direct consideration. The second is the reliability of the measures used to classify venture strategies and industry structures. The third is the nature of the data and the tests used, which do not permit certain analyses that might otherwise be desired.

Research Design and Framework

In using venture capitalists as research sites, I consciously restricted the scope of inquiry to the particular type of new venture that Liles described as the "high-potential venture." Such a venture "is started with the *intention* that it grow rapidly in sales and profits and become a large corporation."[22] Given their intention, it is to be expected that the sampled ventures would approach markets and competition more aggressively than would the more common, "consciously underachieving" venture that exists primarily to provide a wage or salary for its owner.[23] In particular, the ventures in this sample would probably use differentiated strategies, with their broad scope and resource-consuming distinctive competences, both more frequently and more effectively than would conscious underachievers. Because of the numerous likely differences between this sample and other types of new ventures, the findings are not intended to apply to the latter.[24]

A second source of limitations was the exclusion of macroeconomic variables from the conceptual framework of new venture performance. Although statistical tests of the sample did not reveal performance differences associated with the year of a venture's founding, the possibility of such effects cannot be ruled out. The sample appears to be generally free of industries that are notoriously cyclical or sensitive to interest rates. Airlines and coal mining might represent such industries, but the experiences of the one airline and two coal mining ventures in this sample suggest that other effects also were at work. Interestingly, the airline failed despite declining interest rates and an economic recovery and the two coal mining ventures each operated unsuccessfully despite the advantage of an Arab oil embargo during their startup years. The diversity of the sample and of the years covered for different ventures suggest that no systematic macroeconomic bias was injected.

Measures Used

The classifications of strategy and of industry structure were made carefully but subjectively by me. Despite the use of published material, data from venture business plans, discussion with industry experts, and an independent expert's participation in strategy classification, the findings remain dependent on my judgment. Although a venture or industry could have been misclassified, there appears to be no possibility of systematic error in the classifications. Random error would reduce the level of significance but not change the direction of significant or near-significant differences.

Even if proposed business strategies are accurately identified from the venture's business plan, a fundamental limitation remains. There is the possibility that ventures did not put into practice the strategies that they proposed. (Gross discrepancies are unlikely, however. A recent survey of entrepreneurs reported that 89 percent of their companies use their business plan to set management and employee performance goals and evaluation standards.)[25] The undesirability of relying on retrospective descriptions of strategy has been discussed in chapter 5, but the resultant tradeoff must be recognized.

It sometimes is argued that small, owner-managed companies strongly reflect the objectives and values of their owner. Such companies are said to be very flexible, even opportunistic, in nimbly negotiating a complex environment. New ventures share the traits of smallness, owner-management, and seeming flexibility, and are somewhat experimental, too. Thus it might be expected that new ventures would be likely to abandon a less successful strategy in favor of a more promising one. Their early version of a business plan might bear little resemblance to the strategy they enacted.

This argument may have merit, but it clearly runs afoul of countervailing forces in the case of the typical high-potential venture that has obtained venture capital. The mere acts of reducing a strategy to writing and presenting it to one's backers may stimulate greater commitment to it on the part of the entrepreneur. More important, though, is the effect of the venture capitalist. In both the literature and the field interviews conducted for this research, venture capitalists generally confirmed the significance they attach to strategy. A plausible strategy is a key selling point in securing financing. Moreover, participating venture capitalists typically take directors' positions, and may enjoy a supermajority on the board during some specified early period. Thus, they are in a position to prevent capricious or imprudent modification of the strategy that they initially endorsed.

Even if a new venture substantially changes its strategy during its first several years, its performance often will be weaker than a venture that initially chose a more suitable strategy. Not only is there likely to be a period of mediocre or unsuccessful performance that triggers the change, but the costs of repositioning the company are likely to weaken financial performance during and even after the change.

Thus the results of an inappropriate initial strategy may be mitigated, but are unlikely to be overcome, by an opportune revision of that strategy. The three-to-five year range of data used for the sample ventures further reduces the likelihood of the strategy being changed soon enough to alter substantially the venture's performance classification. Even so, the findings concerning the effectiveness of strategies should be received with some caution in view of the possibility of subsequent shifts in strategy.

A parallel concern arises from the importance of strategy implementation. It is quite likely that in some situations an appropriate strategy brought unhappy results largely because of poor implementation. Like most strategic management research on the strategy–performance relationship, this research can only acknowledge the role of implementation. More than some, it has taken into account the characteristics of managers (here, the entrepreneurs) as possible determinants of performance. It was thought that prior experience as an entrepreneur or as a manager in a related industry would improve an entrepreneur's effectiveness. No significant performance effect was found, though, suggesting at a minimum that effective implementation skills remain uncaptured by the measures used. In this shortcoming my research would join the bulk of the strategic management literature on strategy implementation.[26]

It is also possible that certain strategies are inherently more difficult than others to implement. This is an issue quite distinct from the other implementation issues, though, since if the difficulty inheres in the strategy it perforce becomes an inseparable element of the strategy, to be taken into account whenever risk–reward calculations are made by strategists. The entrepreneur may be presumed to be able to overcome the difficulty more easily if he possesses certain attributes—but this returns the argument to the bailiwick of the researchers in entrepreneurship, where only modest progress has been made.

In sum, caution must be exercised in considering the findings of this research because of the likely (but unmeasured) impact of the entrepreneur's implementation skills on new venture performance under any given strategy. The impact could be greater or weaker for different strategies, too. This research has not succeeded in associating experience, age, or education with performance, and can only fall back on the so-called "amalgam" of subjective assessments that guide venture capitalists.

Nature of the Data and Tests Used

The major limitation imposed by the data and tests used is an inability to measure the magnitude of differences between subsamples. The Mann–Whitney *U* test and Spearman rank correlations used in this research permit conclusions as to the existence of a statistically significant difference, but cannot measure its size.

To appreciate more fully the nature of this limitation, suppose a statistically significant performance difference is found to exist when ventures are classified according to some criterion. Neither the magnitude of the difference nor the proportion of total variance in venture performance accounted for by the variable in question can be determined through the tests used in this research. It is possible that a statistically significant performance difference is too small to justify the information costs of classification.

A more important limitation also arises from the inability to measure differences. When confronted with a choice between a venture that conforms to one but flouts another of the statistically supported propositions, and another venture that flouts the first proposition but heeds the second, an analyst would like to know which proposition is more important. Unfortunately, it is not possible to compare the performance differences attributable to the two propositions based on the statistical tests used.

A further data and test limitation affects the multiple-factor propositions. Since there is no analysis of variance, it is impossible to say which of two factors played the greater role in causing a statistically significant performance difference. For example, it is impossible to say whether strategy or stage had the greater effect on the results of the strategy–stage propositions.

In chapter 7 suggestions will be offered to extend this research. Inasmuch as the present research was intended to identify those factors that significantly affect new venture performance and to prepare the way for subsequent research based on the model proposed and refined here, the limitations discussed above do not appear to pose insuperable obstacles to further progress in building a strategic management theory of new venture performance.

Summary

The research results developed in this chapter strongly support the use of a contingency approach to strategies for new ventures. On the basis of existing theory on new ventures and entrepreneurship, in strategic management, and in industrial organization economics, it seemed likely that both new venture business strategy and industry structure would affect new venture performance. Tests of various one-factor propositions lent credibility to the claims of importance for both strategy and industry structure, but did not establish any significant effects for the characteristics of the entrepreneur that were examined.

Following the lead of recent strategic management research, the concept of industry evolution was used to capture concisely these industry structural factors. Paired with venture business strategy, this provided a useful set of prescriptions for new venture strategy.

The prescriptions were summarized in a two-by-two matrix. Breadth of strategic scope (broad vs. narrow) and stage of industry evolution (early vs. late) provided the bases for classification. Ventures were found to perform better when broad scopes were paired with early stages or when narrow scopes were used in late-stage industries.

The results and interpretations presented in this chapter produced a foundation for further research toward a contingency theory of new venture performance. They also provided the basis for improved understanding and decisions by entrepreneurs and venture capitalists. Implications for research and for practitioners will be discussed in chapter 7.

Notes

1. Karl H. Vesper, *New Venture Strategies* (Englewood Cliffs, N.J.: Prentice-Hall, 1980).

2. Michael E. Porter, *Competitive Strategy* (New York: Free Press, 1980).

3. Derek F. Abell, *Defining the Business: The Starting Point of Strategic Planning* (Englewood Cliffs, N.J.: Prentice-Hall, 1980).

4. Sidney Siegel, *Nonparametric Statistics for the Behavioral Sciences* (New York: McGraw-Hill, 1956), p. 271.

5. William M. Hoad and Peter Rosko, *Management Factors Contributing to the Success and Failure of New Small Manufacturers* (Ann Arbor, Mich.: Bureau of Business Research, University of Michigan, 1964).

6. Orvis F. Collins and David G. Moore, *The Enterprising Man* (East Lansing, Mich.: Michigan State University, 1964); Lawrence M. Lamont, "What Entrepreneurs Learn from Experience," *Journal of Small Business Management* 10 (July 1972):36–41; Vesper, *New Venture Strategies.*

7. Norman Raymond Smith, *The Entrepreneur and His Firm: The Relationship Between Type of Man and Type of Company* (Ann Arbor, Mich.: Bureau of Business Research, University of Michigan, 1964); James W. Carland, Frank Hoy, William R. Boulton, and Jo Ann C. Carland, "Differentiating Entrepreneurs from Small Business Owners: A Conceptualization," *Academy of Management Review* 9 (1984):354–359.

8. Hoad and Rosko, *Success and Failure.*

9. Robert H. Brockhaus, "Psychology of the Entrepreneur," paper presented at the Conference on Research and Education in Entrepreneurship, St. Louis University, March 1980, Robert H. Brockhaus, "Risk-Taking Propensity of Entrepreneurs," *Academy of Management Journal* 23 (1980):509–520.

10. Porter, *Competitive Strategy,* p. 35.

11. E. Ralph Biggadike, *Corporate Diversification: Entry, Strategy, and Performance* (Boston: Graduate School of Business, Harvard University, 1979).

12. Abell, *Defining the Business.*

13. Charles W. Hofer, "Toward a Contingency Theory of Business Strategy," *Academy of Management Journal* 18 (1975):784–810. A number of examples are provided in chapter 3.

14. George S. Yip, *Barriers to Entry: A Corporate-Strategy Perspective* (Lexington, Mass.: Lexington Books, 1982), p. 129.

15. Ibid., p. 37.

16. Charles W. Hofer and Dan E. Schendel, *Strategy Formulation: Analytical Concepts* (St. Paul, Minn.: West Publishing Co., 1978).

17. Porter, *Competitive Strategy.*

18. Hofer and Schendel, *Strategy Formulation.*

19. Carl R. Anderson and Carl P. Zeithaml, "Stage of the Product Life Cycle, Business Strategy, and Business Performance," *Academy of Management Journal* 27 (1984):5–24.

20. Hofer, "Toward a Contingency Theory"; Anderson and Zeithaml, "Stage of the Product Life Cycle."

21. Abell, *Defining the Business.*

22. Patrick R. Liles, *New Business and the Entrepreneur* (Homewood, Ill.: Richard D. Irwin, 1974), p. 4.

23. Jeffrey Susbauer, "Commentary," in *Strategic Management,* edited by Dan E. Schendel and Charles W. Hofer, (Boston: Little, Brown, 1979), pp. 327–332.

24. The distinctions made in my research are quite similar to those made by Carland, Hoy, Boulton, and Carland, "Differentiating Entrepreneurs from Small Business Owners."

7
Implications for Venture Capitalists, Entrepreneurs, and Research

What are the implications of this study for practitioners and for research? Both venture capitalists and entrepreneurs can benefit from the improved understanding of the contingent nature of venture strategy prescriptions and from the deepened appreciation of the importance of industry structural variables. This chapter offers advice to both groups of practitioners.

As far as new venture research is concerned, this book illuminates the relative advantages and disadvantages of the Abell, Porter, and Vesper classification schemes.[1] I comment on each of them and recommend several steps to further the development of a theory of new venture performance. The revised paradigm developed in this study—*NVP* = *f(IS, S, E)*—merits use in future research in this direction. Both limited-domain, contingent theories and frame theories are needed for nearly all aspects of new venture performance. I discuss the research needs and describe a specific research project that will draw more effectively on the wisdom of venture capitalists in developing a theory of new venture performance.

Implications for Practitioners

The results confirm much of the wisdom of venture capitalists and their general "model" of new venture performance. Their widely expressed desires for differentiation and competitive advantage square with the successful performance of differentiated strategies and with the weaker advantage of focused over undifferentiated strategies. Their emphasis on finding niches and segments receives somewhat less clear support, though. Like Biggadike's study of corporate ventures,[2] this research indicates the advantage of broad business definitions.

Differentiated strategies outperformed focused strategies, at least in early stages of industry evolution. Both strategies rely on some aspect of differentiation. The principal difference between the two is their breadth of scope—

the differentiated strategy comprises a broad, even industrywide domain rather than a narrowly focused one. Competitive advantage may be more starkly clear when a venture has tailored itself quite closely to the needs of one niche, but it appears to return less to the venture than does an advantage that transcends the boundaries of one or two niches. Thus through their justifiable search for competitive advantage, venture capitalists may be overlooking the more profitable strategy that has a less obvious, but more widely usable, advantage.

The superiority of strategies that blend differentiation with broader scope may result from several factors. First, a focused strategy may harm a venture's long-term prospects by restricting its scope to one or a few market segments. Among young industries, it is not uncommon for early-developing segments to be surpassed by later segments. Thus an entrant in a development or early growth stage industry may be wise to maintain viable positions in several emerging segments until clearer signs of the industry's probable course of evolution develop. A differentiated strategy enables the venture to compete in multiple segments, provided the distinctive competences are exploitable in each of them.

Second, a differentiated strategy often exposes the venture to a greater variety of customer types and needs than would be encountered in a single segment. This exposure may stimulate the venture to develop additional competences which it could exploit as the industry developed, even if the original segment failed to grow substantially.[3]

Third, considerable potential for growth and profits may exist in applications of distinctive competences to similar market segments. A venture might expand its initial operations through replication of its strategy in a segment related to earlier segments. If so, the difficulty and riskiness of growing should be lessened by the venture's previous experience with its strategy.

The practitioners whose interests are most central to this research are venture capitalists and entrepreneurs. The next two sections discuss the implications of this research for these two groups. They are summarized by tables appearing at the beginning of their respective sections.

Implications for Venture Capitalists

The implications of this research for venture capitalists fall into two areas: (1) there are indications of important performance differences among venture strategies and industry structures; and (2) there are implications about the criteria used by venture capitalists to evaluate investment opportunities. The implications are summarized in table 7–1.

Venture capitalists should be attracted to the broader scope of differentiation strategies because of the increased capital gains that are likely to accompany the significantly greater growth of a successful venture using this

Table 7–1
Key Implications for Venture Capitalists

Strategy and industry structure belong in venture capitalists' investment criteria.
Broadly defined, differentiated strategies perform better than focused strategies in early-stage industries.
Venture capitalists' preferences for focused strategies in mature industries are justified by their performance advantage over broadly defined strategies.
Venture capitalists should resist the temptation to "bet on an industry" by backing an undifferentiated venture in a mature industry.
Subjective assessments of an entrepreneur's traits and track record apparently are more effective than objective biographical data in evaluating a new venture's prospects.

strategy. A focused strategy appears to limit the new venture's potential growth by restricting it to but a few segments. The superior performance of differentiated strategies among early-stage industries should produce larger, more profitable ventures that would be more attractive to institutional and individual investors. This investor interest is important because venture capitalists often dispose of their shares when a venture makes its initial public offering of stock. The venture capitalists' desire for capital gains appears to coincide with the interests of Liles's intendedly large, "high-potential" new venture,[4] and both seem best served by a differentiated strategy.

The advantages of broad scope and extensible distinctive competences may be weakened by industry maturity. Here the venture capitalists' preference for a focused strategy was more emphatic and appears more advisable. New ventures encounter entrenched incumbents when entering mature industries. Often even the smaller segments are targets of differentiation by incumbents, leaving only still more specialized niches for the entrant.

The interviewed venture capitalists would invest in an entrant that could fill a niche in a mature industry, and some would even invest in an undifferentiated venture if they foresaw industrywide improvement through some fundamental change. The findings of this research, however, argue against anything but a focused strategy in entering mature industries. An undifferentiated strategy would afford weak protection against incumbent's expansion if a mature industry suddenly were revitalized, anyway. Thus venture capitalists would do well to heed their own wisdom and resist the occasional urge to "bet on an industry" that already is mature, and instead limit their new venture investments in such industries to those that propose focused strategies. Only the clear existence of disequilibrium might override this advice.

There are also implications for venture capitalists in the nonsignificance of the effects of entrepreneurs' characteristics. Venture capitalists are nearly unanimous in assigning the greatest importance to the entrepreneur rather than to the venture's strategy or industry. Although no biographic data were found to be related to performance differences, some key aspects of the entrepreneur's track record were not tested in this study. The most noteworthy omission may have been the degree of success represented by an entrepreneur's prior experience. "Years of experience" were used to account objectively for the characteristics of entrepreneurs because it would have been impossible to interview or otherwise examine most of the entrepreneurs. Even had interviews or other contact been possible, it would have been impossible to determine the entrepreneur's characteristics as they had existed years earlier. This is a fundamental difficulty in researching the characteristics of successful entrepreneurs, as explained in chapter 3.

Venture capitalists, of course, assess the caliber of the entrepreneur largely through an evaluation of his or her track record. No attempt was made to query the cooperating venture capitalists as to their actual evaluations of the sample's entrepreneurs because the years of postevaluation venture performance might have clouded or colored many people's recollections of their former impressions. In only a few cases were such evaluations found in surviving notes or memos written by the venture capitalists. Thus no data were available on what most venture capitalists would say is their first and foremost consideration.

The failure to find significant performance differences associated with age, education, or years of a variety of experiences has removed most objective measurements from further consideration here. An exception must be made for the psychological tests that have been used to describe, identify, or preselect successful entrepreneurs. Locus-of-control beliefs at startup have been found to differentiate successful from unsuccessful entrepreneurs, albeit in a sample of less ambitious ventures.[5] The limitations on extending this conclusion to more ambitious ventures have been noted in chapter 3, but it remains possible that venture capitalists could profit from testing the locus-of-control beliefs of prospective entrepreneurs. Apart from locus-of-control, there has been scant success in relating psychology to entrepreneurial success in ways that offer predictive value.[6]

If psychological tests and objective biographic data offer little help, perhaps venture capitalists are right to rely on their subjective appraisals of entrepreneurs' track records. Whether these appraisals are more valuable than evaluations of strategy and industry structure cannot be determined at this point. It seems likely that there are some characteristics which ought to serve as virtually automatic disqualifiers of an entrepreneur, particularly when venture capitalists have to decide where to allocate their own scarce analytical talents and time among dozens of proposals. Among the entrepreneurs good enough to survive such an initial screening, it is possible that those deemed to have good track records have learned through experience, or perhaps sensed from the beginning, what types of strategy are appropriate, either in general or in particular situations. If this is true, the venture capitalist and the strategy researcher are approaching the same factor via two different routes.

Even in the case of an experienced entrepreneur whose track record is acceptable, however, the venture capitalist may be better advised to make an independent assessment of the proposed venture's strategy than to take its suitability for granted. Recent reports of venture capitalists becoming increasingly involved in the management of troubled investees[7] suggest still another reason for them to hone their skills in evaluating strategies. These reports indicate two possibilities: (1) venture capitalists are not so skilled at choosing entrepreneurs on the basis of track record and personal characteristics to be able to rely on those criteria alone; or (2) regardless of their skills in choosing entrepreneurs, questions of strategy and industry structure loom more important than venture capitalists had supposed.

Implications for Entrepreneurs

If venture capitalists can benefit from enhanced understanding of the effects of strategy and industry structure on new venture performance, one would expect entrepreneurs to find something of value, too. After all, both have a strong interest in the performance of their new ventures and in avoiding ventures that are likely to fail.

Not surprisingly then, the implications for entrepreneurs are similar to those for venture capitalists and most of them concern strategies and industry structure. The implications for entrepreneurs are summarized in table 7–2.

The financial and opportunity costs of a venture begin before the entrepreneur approaches venture capitalists and cannot be avoided if a venture is to reach even the proposal stage. Moreover, the entrepreneur will have a better chance of obtaining funds if the venture proposal seems feasible. An improved knowledge of what affects new venture performance thus has obvious value to the entrepreneur.

The inconclusive findings concerning the entrepreneur's characteristics already have been described and discussed. As our attention shifts to the implications for entrepreneurs, there is another issue to consider. The venture capitalist can always decline to back a venture and seek a better alternative if the entrepreneur seems unqualified, but the entrepreneur who is unsuited to his would-be vocation faces a less comfortable choice. If the entrepreneur's unsuitability stems from a lack of training or experience, it is possible (although not always practical) to acquire it. If the entrepreneur is psychologically unsuited for entrepreneurship, on the other hand, it may be impossible to alter the fact. (Research has not established the effectiveness of psychological training programs in improving the entrepreneurial fitness of individuals,

Table 7–2
Key Implications for Entrepreneurs

Venture strategy and industry structure ought to be key factors in an entrepreneur's planning of a venture.
Broadly defined, differentiated strategies perform better than focused strategies in early-stage industries.
Early-stage industries are more attractive for entry than are late-stage industries.
New ventures are more successful in industries that have heterogeneous products.
New venture performance is improved by industry disequilibrium and barriers to entry that are likely to rise.

as discussed in chapter 3.) In either event the entrepreneur, unlike the venture capitalist, is likely to be denied participation in a successful new venture.

Since this research failed to find any significant performance differences related to the entrepreneur, its implications for the entrepreneur lie in the strategy and industry structure propositions. Essentially the same points can be made here as in the previous section: (1) differentiated strategies outperform focused strategies in early stages of industry evolution, which also is the better time to enter an industry; (2) if entering a mature industry, use a focused strategy; and (3) present disequilibrium and subsequent barriers to entry enhance new venture performance. The entrepreneur's limited alternatives for entrepreneurial activity and high personal stake in a venture's success create an incentive to design a strategy and choose an industry carefully.

Molding the proposed strategy is the entrepreneur's responsibility. Care in planning can save the costs and risks of strategic change early in a venture's life. Thus the entrepreneur should take pains to develop a desirable strategy before startup, before the venture's initial resources have been invested or otherwise committed to a particular deployment pattern. A distinctive competence should be identified, and plans made to develop and exploit it, since ventures appear to be more successful when using the competence-based strategies (that is, differentiated and focused strategies).

Assuming the entrepreneur possesses the requisite knowledge and understanding of an industry, he should seek one that satisfies the industry structure criteria suggested earlier. In particular, industries are most attractive if their products are heterogeneous. Entrepreneurs apparently find greater receptiveness for specialization and greater insulation from scale-dependent price competition when customers already appreciate (and pay for) differentiated products. This advice is not new, but the additional recommendation to differentiate broadly rather than narrowly is a departure from much of the literature. Yet for the presumably ambitious new ventures that made up this sample, the differentiated strategy proved superior to the focused strategy. In seeking bases for differentiation, at least in early-stage industries, the entrepreneur might do well to yield to the temptation to dream, or at least to think expansively.

Implications for Research

The results of this research indicate that new venture performance is determined in part by the venture's strategy and by industry structural factors. Although it was impossible to measure the magnitudes, both had significant effects. Thus, the results support the revised paradigm of new venture performance, $NVP = f(IS, S, E)$.

These findings have important implications for new venture research, which are summarized in table 7–3. Most obvious is the argument for incorporating venture business strategy and industry structure into future research on new venture performance. The literature review in chapter 3 did not uncover such research on independent (as opposed to corporate) new ventures. In this respect, new venture theory and research in 1985 resemble the business policy theory and research of 10 or 15 years earlier. Considerable work remains if new venture research is to attain even the state reached by business policy–strategic management. The path may well parallel that of the policy field, as the tasks are quite similar.

This book was conceived as theory-building research. It sought to refine the existing conception and understanding of entrepreneurship (that is, $NVP = f[E]$) by adding the insights of the Austrian school of economics concerning disequilibrium and the entrepreneur's role in its elimination. It also sought to integrate these Austrian insights with the more conventional and empiricist theories of industrial organization economics to capture the effects of industry structure on new venture performance.

The addition of venture business strategy completed the theoretical map and paradigm: $NVP = f(IS, S, E)$. Despite pioneering work by Vesper,[8] little new venture research had taken account of even the most basic generic strategies for new ventures.[9]

The potential value of incorporating strategy in any framework or model of new venture performance was indicated by the results of propositions 3 through 6. The most significant difference ($p < .075$) was obtained in testing Porter's generic strategies of industrywide differentiation and focus in proposition 3. When Abell's definitions of differentiated and focused strategies were used in proposition 5, reported significance declined ($p < .165$).

Based on my experience in conducting this research, I have reached several conclusions on the relative strengths and weaknesses of the Porter, Abell, and Vesper classification schemes.[10] It appears that each offers advantages that depend on the research purpose on hand.

First, Porter's generic strategies are not inclusive of all businesses. In this

Table 7–3
Key Implications for Research

A new paradigm, relating venture performance to strategy and industry structure as well as to the entrepreneur, suggests that future research on new venture performance should include these variables.
Porter's classification of strategies does not adequately describe differentiation and omits many undifferentiated strategies.
Abell's classification of strategies does not fully distinguish low-cost from undifferentiated strategies.
Vesper's entry wedges are useful but not sufficient for classifying new venture strategies.
A classification scheme that integrates the above-mentioned schemes yields significant performance differences between categories.
Future research should develop both limited domain and frame theories of new venture performance.
Future research should investigate the decision criteria of venture capitalists.

Sources: Michael E. Porter, *Competitive Strategy: Techniques for Analyzing Industries and Competitors* (New York: Free Press, 1980); Derek F. Abell, *Defining the Business: The Starting Point of Strategic Planning* (Englewood Cliffs, N.J.: Prentice-Hall, 1980); Karl H. Vesper, *New Venture Strategies* (Englewood Cliffs, N.J.: Prentice-Hall, 1980).

book, 5 of 17 ventures did not fit any of Porter's 3 strategies. The strategies of these ventures had broad, industrywide targets (and thus were not focus strategies), but had sought no cost advantage or differentiation, and thus could not be classified as either low-cost or differentiated. According to Porter, "the firm failing to develop its strategy in at least one of the three directions—a firm that is 'stuck in the middle'—is in an extremely poor strategic position."[11]

Thus Porter's three generic strategies are not *intended* to describe all business units. Researchers who somehow force an entire sample into the three categories have probably misclassified some of the business units.

Porter appears to offer an important distinction that eludes the researcher who relies on Abell. Abell used "undifferentiated" to describe the strategies that combined a broad market and an absence of differentiation by customer group, customer function, or technology.[12] This offers the advantage of including the strategyless businesses that are omitted by Porter's scheme, but does so only at the cost of lumping them with the pure cost competitor.

The distinction thereby lost by Abell is one worth retaining, since firms with broad customer-group and customer-function definitions may enjoy economies of scale. Lacking the volume to gain scale economies, an entrant may attain a low-cost position through new or improved technologies or processes. In my research, however, the strategyless new ventures lacked the volume that might have yielded scale economies and pursued no other means to achieve cost advantages. Having also failed to pursue differentiation, they were left with no source of competitive advantage whatsoever. In Abell's terminology, such firms were "undifferentiated"; in Porter's terminology, they were "stuck in the middle" from their very inception.

A second difference between the two schemes concerns their treatment of differentiation. As was noted in chapter 6, Abell had in mind several ways of differentiating, including the differentiation of a company's products across market segments. To Porter, differentiation meant creating a difference that is recognized *industrywide*. In the sample studied here, one venture met Abell's definition of differentiation while failing to meet Porter's. In this case, the venture also sought a low-cost position through a secondary strategy. A secondary strategy is not necessary, however, and this venture would have been unclassifiable by Porter's scheme had it not had one. Note that while the venture quite clearly had a strategy, without its secondary strategy it would have fallen into the unclassified, "stuck in the middle" group. The five other ventures in that group were undifferentiated, strategyless ventures that approached their markets in ways that diverged substantially from the strategy of this venture. Thus Abell's classification scheme, through its richer, more sophisticated understanding of differentiation, makes distinctions that would be impossible with Porter's scheme.

Third, Abell's richer detailing and distinctions among differentiation strategies should be helpful to researchers who wish to investigate differences among alternative approaches to differentiation. Abell treated these differences conceptually and theoretically, but they have not been addressed in new venture research.

In sum, Abell's classification scheme deals with differentiated strategies more effectively than Porter's scheme and avoids excluding or misclassifying the venture that attempts to differentiate other than through a single, industrywide difference. Porter's scheme has the advantage of distinguishing low-cost strategies from undifferentiated strategies. Relatively few examples will be found of new ventures relying on economies of scale, so Abell's appears the better of the two schemes for new venture researchers. A combination of the two seems feasible, as it essentially requires only that one additional distinction be made in Abell's scheme.

New venture researchers have special classification needs that are not satisfied by general-purpose schemes such as Porter's or Abell's. For this reason the entry wedges of Vesper [13] were adapted to the needs of this book. His supply shortage wedge accurately describes many of the undifferentiated, "strategyless" ventures that are inadequately classified by either Porter or Abell. In addition, the political substrategies (customer contract, favored purchasing, rules changes) drawn from Vesper's entry wedges capture a dimension that eludes other generic strategy classification schemes. Although they did not appear frequently enough among this sample to be tested in this study, they seem to merit further attention.

Despite the classificatory value of the entry wedges, Vesper's scheme would not be sufficient by itself. The main entry wedges used in this book (new product or service and parallel competition) and the other two identified by Vesper (franchising and acquisition of a going concern) do not, for example, distinguish among differentiated, industrywide cost-based, undifferentiated, and focused strategies. My research has demonstrated the significant performance differences between some of these strategy categories. Thus the Vesper entry wedges seem most useful as supplements to stronger, more comprehensive strategy classifications based on works such as Abell and Porter.

Directions for Future Research

This book was conceived and carried out as an effort to build theory. Having developed a revised framework of new venture performance by synthesizing theory and research from the entrepreneurship, strategic management, and industrial organization fields, it was necessary to seek preliminary confirmation or refutation of the framework. Thus 19 propositions, developed from the framework, were subjected to statistical tests. The findings provided noteworthy confirmation and point to the new paradigm, $NVP = f(IS, S, E)$.

Thus, new venture theory has been shifted from its earlier state of uncertainty or even ignorance concerning the possible role of strategy and industry structure in determining new venture performance. The next research steps should consist of the development and testing of hypotheses in the several areas covered by the new paradigm. Several research activities and lines of inquiry would contribute to these steps.

First, researchers need a common vocabulary and concepts of new venture strategy. One contribution of this book has been to pull together diverse models and to develop from them a usable model of new venture performance. The Abell, Hofer and Schendel, and Vesper approaches to strategy have been combined and found to provide a basis for classifying new venture strategies.[14] The independent expert and I reached initial agreement on about three-quarters of the 17 strategy classifications that were necessary here, but further research could benefit from a less subjective method.

The strategic management field provides an example of the benefits and potential risks of quantifying strategy. Considerable effort has gone into this task since Hatten first used regression techniques to capture strategy and establish the existence of strategic groups within an industry.[15] Harrigan has provided a recent example of the type of quantification that would benefit new venture performance research. She proposed a scheme of vertical integration strategies, identified the key dimensions along which the strategies varied, and developed indices for measuring each.[16]

An analogous accomplishment would be the development of indices to measure a venture's position along Abell's dimensions of business definition, including the venture's type and degree of differentiation.[17] These would encourage consistency among diverse research projects and would increase the researcher's ability to identify the critical components of new venture strategies in various settings. For example, one could seek answers to the question, Are there important differences in performance between ventures that differentiate on the basis of technology used and those that differentiate on the basis of customer group served or customer function performed?

Second, new venture researchers should begin to include industry structure in their research designs. New venture performance has been shown to be related not only to an industry's stage of evolution (which may be said to have captured the industry's growth rate, a widely accepted factor in new venture performance) but also to its product heterogeneity, disequilibrium, and rising barriers to entry. These are industry structural variables.

Industry structural variables are not unknown in the study of entry, of course. Yip's examination and modification of entry barrier theory serves as an example of their importance.[18] Unfortunately, it does not seem that his method can as yet be applied easily to new ventures. Because he used the PIMS data base, he obtained industry entry data from large incumbents. Such companies may be aware only of successful entries plus the larger failed attempts. (Yip's criterion of a 5-percent market share for inclusion in his sample suggests as much.) They are unlikely to be able to describe smaller entrants' strategies in great detail, either. Thus they are a far less adequate source of information for new venture research than for Yip's purposes.

A study such as Yip's does make use of valuable industry structural data. Researchers using a medium-grained methodology could use such industry-descriptive data to select industry sites within which to seek their samples of new ventures. The generally available PIMS data do not identify participants' industries, though. This means that such researchers could not select samples within whatever PIMS industries they considered to be their structural archetypes. Instead, researchers would probably have to analyze selected industries to fill cells in some model of relevant structural dimensions.[19]

All this presupposes the existence of such a model, which is not the case for new ventures as distinct from other entrants. This study has offered plausible, tested propositions drawn from existing theory and applied to a neglected topic. Thus one contribution is its suggestion of product (and, by implication, strategic) heterogeneity, disequilibrium, and rising barriers to entry as dimensions for classifying industries in subsequent research on new venture performance.

Third, the contingent nature of the strategy–industry structure–performance relationship calls for researchers to pursue both limited-domain, contingency theories and what Rumelt called "frame theories," which identify "the issues or problem areas which are critically important within the chosen context."[20] Limited-domain theories are important in strategic management, as is clear in the frequent references herein to studies of strategies for declining businesses, turnaround situations, low market share businesses, and so forth. The new venture research field now requires the approach taken a decade ago in strategic management.[21] Having accepted that successful new venture performance is not gained through adherence to universal principles, a researcher ought to inquire into the strategic rules governing various new venture contexts. For example, one could examine startups only in mature industries, or only in shakeout industries: How should a venture compete in each of these stages of industry evolution?

The emergence of limited domain theories would aid in the development of frame theories. As more is learned about new venture performance in certain contexts, the question naturally arises, Which variables or factors are of particular significance in specific contexts? As an example of the mutual interests of limited-domain and frame theories, consider the earlier examples of research on new ventures only in mature industries or only in shakeout industries. There are differences between the two stages of evolution, and it seems likely that new ventures would need to pursue somewhat different strategies, or perhaps to pursue strategies somewhat differently. This juxtaposition of words illustrates the point: the differences may be fundamental, in that different variables have significant effects; or they may be differences of degree, in that the same variables matter, but their relative importance or the optimum approach to them, does differ.

Fourth, large gaps remain in our knowledge of the determinants of new venture performance. It has been argued that venture capitalists represent a rather neglected source of wisdom in this regard. Indeed, their "model" anticipated the new paradigm. There is much still to be learned about the wisdom of venture capitalists. Prior research (reviewed in chapter 2) has surveyed venture capitalists to learn their financial policies and investment preferences, their reasons for rejecting proposed ventures, and similar information. Yet there appears to have been no research that used a decision-making exercise rather than a survey to capture venture capitalists' real criteria and their associated weights.[22]

Stahl and Zimmerer used a decision-making exercise to study the corporate acquisition decision process. They noted that their approach allowed them to "incorporate a planned experimental design into the exercise and substantially control the information the participants incorporate into the decisions."[23] Example acquisition candidates were created that had various levels of each criterion covered in the study. Respondents indicated their recommendation regarding each candidate. Stahl and Zimmerer used the responses to regress each respondent's decisions on the criteria.

The result was a regression equation for each respondent and an average relative weight (coefficient) for each criterion across all respondents. The latter data were compared to the "subjective weights" separately assigned to the criteria by the same respondents. Stahl and Zimmerer reported a significant difference between relative (that is, regression-derived) and subjective (that is, self-reported) weights and commented that their decision makers "did not demonstrate good insight" into their own decision criteria.[24]

The implications of Stahl and Zimmerer's research can easily be extended to our knowledge of venture capitalists' decision making. If that knowledge is based almost entirely on self-reports, it may be as flawed as the "subjective" weights reported by Stahl and Zimmerer. The widespread claim that venture capitalists rely most heavily on their assessment of a venture's management is indeed based on self-reports. Yet both market attractiveness and product differentiation ranked as more influential investment decision factors in Tyebjee and Bruno's somewhat more rigorous study.[25] The possibility remains that venture capitalists, too, are poor chroniclers of their own decision making. A research design such as Stahl and Zimmerer used would shed light on this issue and on venture capitalists' real criteria.

Thus the need, rationale, and methodology all are present for a similar research project that would identify the criteria and weights actually used by venture capitalists. Given their apparent success in meeting the test of the marketplace, venture capitalists continue to represent a potentially valuable source of knowledge in the area of new venture performance.

To many of us who undertake research in strategic management, one of the field's principal attractions is its enduring focus on (and foundation in) the "real world." It seems appropriate, then, that I should conclude with a call for using medium-grained methodologies to develop contingency theories of new venture performance, and a call for using decision-making exercises to sharpen our understanding of the criteria actually used by the practitioners of an art that is intimately related to what we wish to study.

Summary

This chapter explored the implications of my research for venture capitalists, entrepreneurs, and researchers. Key implications for each were summarized in tables 7–1, 7–2, and 7–3.

For new venture practitioners (both venture capitalists and entrepreneurs), the advantage of differentiated strategies over focused strategies, at least in early stages of industry evolution, had several implications. Niche-seeking may not be advisable for a venture entering an early-stage industry; a broader business definition appears to offer greater potential exploitation of distinctive competences and a greater probability of competing in market segments that will prove viable in the long run.

Venture capitalists should find broadly defined ventures attractive because of their greater prospects for growth, and hence for capital appreciation. This attractiveness may disappear in entering mature industries, in which focused strategies seem to be superior. Unless disequilibrium can be exploited, venture capitalists should avoid "betting on an industry" that is mature. Finally, venture capitalists' reliance on subjective appraisals of an entrepreneur's track record is not challenged by the objective data analyzed here, as no biographic data had significant effects on venture performance.

Entrepreneurs can benefit from the same strategic implications as venture capitalists, since both types of practitioner profit from new venture success. Particular emphasis was placed on the impact of industry structure on new venture performance, especially on the desirability of product heterogeneity.

Researchers are expected to benefit from the development of a new paradigm of new venture performance, $NVP = f(IS, S, E)$. This research has shown the value of using classifications of venture strategies and industry structures in studying new venture performance. Furthermore, it has suggested the relative advantages and disadvantages of the classifications developed by Abell, Porter, and Vesper. Particularly in comparing Abell and Porter, these advantages and disadvantages have broader implications for strategic management research as well as for new venture research. For new venture researchers, though, Abell appears the better of the two classification schemes. Whichever scheme they choose, new venture researchers would do well to integrate it with Vesper's scheme in order to describe entry wedges more thoroughly.

Several points were made concerning future new venture research directions in light of the new paradigm developed here. First, the type of quantification and the types of research questions that are now appropriate were described. Common vocabularies and classification schemes and indices for measuring ventures' positions along key classificatory dimensions are needed. Second, industry structural variables need to be included in more new venture research. This book suggests product heterogeneity, disequilibrium, and rising entry barriers as important influences on new venture performance. Third, researchers should pursue limited-domain theories that explain performance in various new venture contexts. Finally, venture capitalists are a somewhat neglected source of knowledge on new venture performance. I have proposed a research project to draw more effectively on this resource, inspired in part by the contribution of venture capitalists' wisdom to my own research.

Notes

1. Derek F. Abell, *Defining the Business: The Starting Point of Strategic Planning* (Englewood Cliffs, N.J.: Prentice-Hall, 1980); Michael E. Porter, *Competitive Strategy* (New York: Free Press, 1980); Karl H. Vesper, *New Venture Strategies* (Englewood Cliffs, N.J.: Prentice-Hall, 1980).

2. E. Ralph Biggadike, *Corporate Diversification: Entry, Strategy, and Performance* (Boston: Graduate School of Business, Harvard University, 1979).

3. Discovery of such opportunities is more likely to occur when systematic techniques are applied to the problem. Abell *(Defining the Business)* provides an excellent conceptual guide to mapping types of differentiation and markets. Charles W. Hofer and Dan E. Schendel suggest several techniques for analyzing customer characteristics in *Strategy Formulation: Analytical Techniques* (St. Paul, Minn.: West Publishing Co., 1978).

4. Patrick R. Liles, *New Business and the Entrepreneur* (Homewood, Ill.: Richard D. Irwin, 1974).

5. Robert H. Brockhaus, "Psychology of the Entrepreneur," paper presented at the Conference on Research and Education in Entrepreneurship, St. Louis University, March 1980.

6. Ibid.

7. Michele H. Fleischer, "The Venture Capital 100: Caution is the Word," *Venture* 7 (June 1985):48–56.

8. Vesper, *New Venture Strategies.*

9. In fact, a forerunner of this book has been credited (by William Gartner, "Entry Strategies in an Emerging Industry," *Proceedings, Academy of Management,* edited by Kae H. Chung, (Dallas, Tex., 1983, pp. 413–416) with pointing out the usefulness of Porter's generic strategies in analyzing new ventures' strategies (William R. Sandberg and Charles W. Hofer, "A Strategic Management Perspective on the Determinants of New Venture Success," in *Frontiers of Entrepreneurship Research,* edited by Karl H. Vesper [Wellesley, Mass.: Babson Center for Entrepreneurial Studies, 1982], pp. 204–237).

10. Porter, *Competitive Strategy;* Abell, *Defining the Business;* Vesper, *New Venture Strategies.*

11. Porter, *Competitive Strategy,* p. 41.

12. Abell, *Defining the Business.*

13. Vesper, *New Venture Strategies.*

14. Abell, *Defining the Business;* Hofer and Schendel, *Strategy Formulation;* Vesper, *New Venture Strategies.*

15. Kenneth J. Hatten, "Strategic Models in the Brewing Industry," Ph.D. diss., West Lafayette, Ind.: Purdue University, 1974.

16. Kathryn Rudie Harrigan, *Strategies for Vertical Integration* (Lexington, Mass.: Lexington Books, 1983).

17. Abell, *Defining the Business.*

18. George S. Yip, *Barriers to Entry: A Corporate-Strategy Perspective* (Lexington, Mass.: Lexington Books, 1982).

19. Kathryn Rudie Harrigan is especially instructive on this problem. See her "Research Methodologies for Contingency Approaches to Business Strategy," *Academy of Management Review* 8 (1983):398–405; also see *Strategies for Vertical Integration* for an example of her research method.

20. Richard Rumelt, "Evaluation of Strategy: Theory and Models," in *Strategic Management,* edited by Dan E. Schendel and Charles W. Hofer, (Boston: Little, Brown, 1979), p. 210.

21. Charles W. Hofer, "Toward a Contingency Theory of Business Strategy," *Academy of Management Journal* 18 (1975):784–810.

22. Even Tyebjee and Bruno did not use a decision making exercise. Their survey asked each venture capitalist to report the evaluations and ultimate recommendation made on one or more ventures of the participant's own choosing. Thus there was no basis for comparing the recommendations of two or more venture capitalists on the same venture(s). See Tyzoon T. Tyebjee and Albert V. Bruno, "A Model of Venture Capitalist Investment Activity," *Management Science* 30 (1984):1051–1066.

23. Michael J. Stahl and Thomas W. Zimmerer, "Modeling Strategic Acquisition Decisions: A Simulation of Executives' Acquisition Decisions," *Academy of Management Journal* 27 (1984):372.

24. Ibid., p. 376.

25. As noted earlier, the methodological weaknesses of Tyebjee and Bruno ("A Model of Venture Capitalist Investment Activity") prevent our giving full credence to its rankings. Despite its weaknesses, though, it may be sounder than research based on self-reporting.

Appendix A
Venture Data Form

Venture Name ______________________ Source ____________________
Location _____________ Industry ___________ Start Yr. _______
Venture Capitalist's Investment Mfg Svc Whlsl Retail Finance
Amount _______________________
Type _________________________

THE ENTREPRENEUR'S CHARACTERISTICS AT STARTUP

Sex: M F Race: Cau Black Oriental Hispanic Other ________
Age _____

Education: { Years of College ___ Highest Degree ___ Field ___________ | No College ____ }

Type of Experience	Number of Years										
Managerial	0	1	2	3	4	5	6	7	8	9	10+
Mgr. in similar ind.	0	1	2	3	4	5	6	7	8	9	10+
Entrepreneur	0	1	2	3	4	5	6	7	8	9	10+

Functional Experience:

Accounting Finance Marketing Operations/Production Engineering

Prior Entrepreneurial Experience? { YES ______ SUCCESS MARGINAL FAILURE
Related to this venture? Yes No
NO ______ }

Venture Capitalist's Assessment of Entrepreneur (judgments expressed, adjectives used, etc.)

CHARACTERISTICS OF THE INDUSTRY

Are there barriers to entry? __________ technology capital brand names legal restrictions other ________

Is the market segmented? __________ geography product quality price customer type other ________

Relative to the number of firms in the industry, are there MANY / FEW suppliers?
MANY / FEW customers?

Is rivalry strong? YES NO
If yes, what is the evidence?

If not, why not?

How does the five-year growth rate of the industry compare to the GNP?
Higher _____
Same _____
Lower _____
How has the growth rate changed from the previous five years?

BASED ON THIS AND OTHER INFORMATION, WHAT STAGE OF EVOLUTION DESCRIBES THE INDUSTRY?

Pre-commercial Development Growth Shakeout Maturity Saturation Decline

VENTURE BUSINESS STRATEGY

Total capitalization at startup __________ Pct. equity __________

Which of Vesper's entry wedges are to be used?

Other Entry Wedges	Vesper's Main Entry Wedges: New Product or Service	Vesper's Main Entry Wedges: Parallel Competition
Exploiting partial momentum		
Geographical transfer		
Supply shortage		
Tapping unutilized resources		
Customer sponsorship		
Customer contract		
Becoming second source		
Incumbent company's ceding		
Market relinquishment		
Governmental sponsorship		
Favored purchasing		
Rule changes		
Combinations		

Which of Porter's generic strategies is to be used?

PRICE DIFFERENTIATION FOCUS NONE APPARENT

Evidence?

What distinctive competences are to be developed? (List and explain.)

For each, indicate whether it is to be provided by ENTREPRENEUR, OTHER MANAGEMENT ALREADY ON BOARD, MANAGEMENT YET TO BE HIRED, PURCHASE OF MATERIALS OR INTANGIBLES, or by UNSPECIFIED MEANS.

What objectives are stated, if any? (Give objective, criterion, time frame)

Has the sponsorship or support of others been secured? Who? How? For what?

VENTURE PERFORMANCE

	Years from Startup (197_)							
	1	2	3	4	5	6	7	8
Sales								
Net Income								
Cash Flow								
ROE								
Market Share								
Other ________								

How does this performance compare to the objectives stated earlier?

What was the disposition of the Venture Capitalist's holdings at the close of data?

(REMEMBER: Try to obtain balance sheet data for at least the two most recent years.)

Appendix B
Descriptions of Venture Strategies

Venture A: Oil and Gas Drilling

The venture acquired rigs and entered the oil and gas well contract drilling business, seeking day-rate contracts of one year or more in duration. The company was prepared to work in Texas, Louisiana, and nearby Gulf Coast states. The two partners worked together in a successful drilling company, one as a vice-president (he had an M.B.A. and a B.S.M.E.) and the other as operations manager. Their rigs would be of a standard type used in the industry and there were no stated plans to offer unusual services. The venture was established in 1978 in anticipation of increased drilling activity following the decontrol of oil prices.

Venture B: Oil and Gas Drilling and Workover

The venture purchased and leased rigs and barges and began doing business in the inland waterways of the Gulf Coast region in January, 1980. In addition to drilling, the company provided workover services (pulling out everything in the well, cleaning the bore, replacing pipe and parts as necessary, and restoring the well to production). The founder expected that the company's rigs would perform mostly drilling services during the first two-and-a-half years of operation, then shift somewhat to the less profitable workover market as necessary if drilling activity were to slacken once the market adjusted to decontrol.

The venture partners had worked with the major customers in the Gulf Coast region while employed by the region's leading competitor and believed their credentials were widely recognized. They anticipated having lower costs than the industry norm because they were acquiring all new rigs and would employ experienced crews.

The company's three owned and four leased rigs would place it fifth among 24 firms in the region. The leader had 16 rigs and the top 8 firms together had 45 of the 104 rigs then being operated in the region. Rig utilization by the 3 largest competitors reportedly was extremely high (97–98 percent) in 1977–79.

The venture partners expected increased drilling activity through 1981, which would permit barges to work more regularly in drilling than they usually would. They saw workover as a means to create drilling opportunities by developing a customer base.

Venture C: Providing Casing Crews and Drilling Equipment

Founded in 1976, this venture provided casing crews, which were needed two or three times for each well drilled; drilling tools; and diesel-powered drive hammers for driving pipe in preparation for drilling wells.

Larger competitors carried larger and broader inventories of tools and pipe and therefore were able to handle a wider range of customer needs and customer types. The venture did not inventory pipe and thus was not able to win jobs with the larger, independent oil companies. Instead, it relied on its founder's 30 years of experience in drilling and in running casing crews. Since customers paid for the crews by the foot (plus standby time), a casing job's profitability depended on a crew's working efficiently during the available working time. If, for reasons not the fault of the customer, a job took longer than expected, the company might not make a profit on it.

No differences were expected between the venture and its competitors insofar as equipment performance, wage rates, or hourly operating costs were concerned.

Venture D: Coal Mining

This venture was established in 1974 to acquire five-year lease rights on coal mining acreage in West Virginia and to buy out (that is, extinguish) another party's marketing contract for the output of the acreage. This would leave the venture free to sell its coal elsewhere. The venture proposed to enter into five-year contracts with two buyers to take its output at a fixed price per ton plus certain cost adjustments. The new owners would hire the current operator to run the mine for ten years.

Historically, earnings of the mines on this acreage, as elsewhere, had followed the spot market price for coal. Even vastly increased output could not overcome major price slumps. The venture's backers believed the price of coal would rise sharply as a result of the "oil shock" that had hit the United States and Western Europe in 1973.

Venture E: Coal Mining

In 1979 the venturers believed that coal prices would rise dramatically as a result of the second "oil crisis," which had hit the United States that year. They moved quickly and by the end of the year managed to acquire an operating property in West Virginia. They intended to hire experienced management and to sell their coal in the customary manner, either by contract or in the spot market. There were no outstanding contracts of significant size or duration, and the founders considered the acquisition a method of avoiding the time, cost, and uncertainty of exploration for coal.

Venture F: Railroad Freight Car Leasing

This venture commenced operations in 1978 as an owner and lessor of railroad hopper cars. The cars were open-top hoppers specially built to haul rock aggregates. To the average person they resembled the traditional "coal car," but the cars differed somewhat in design and in how their loads were dumped. Other types of hopper could also haul aggregate, but not as efficiently. The cars were to be provided on short-term leases to shippers of aggregate. Railroads were not customers of the venture; in fact, they were competitors since they had fleets of hopper cars that they provided at a charge.

The hopper cars were leased at a standard per diem rate. Utilization was the key to success, but the entrepreneur believed this posed no problem in 1978. First, the railroad-owned hopper fleet had declined at a 2 percent annual rate during the past decade and now appeared to be shrinking even more rapidly. Second, a revived coal industry demanded more of the remaining fleet than most rail managements had expected. The result was a hopper shortage that had led the Interstate Commerce Commission to order railroads to provide "equitable service" to all customers. Even important shippers could not secure a guaranteed supply of hoppers from the railroads. Nonrailroad owners were under no such obligation and gladly leased cars to major shippers and others who depended on reliable availability.

The venture's opportunities were further enlarged by a strictly intrastate advantage, too. The state railroad commission required railroads to charge one-third more to haul hoppers they provided than to haul shipper-supplied hoppers. (Furthermore, the ICC required railroads to pay shippers a flat rate per mile for using shipper-supplied cars.) The state commission had declined the railroads' petitions to reduce the rate spread.

The venture planned to lease its owned fleet of special-purpose hoppers to shippers of aggregate located almost exclusively in one state. The entrepreneur also intended to offer car management and maintenance services to investors who wished to own and lease, but not directly manage, hopper cars.

Most of the leases were expected to result from the entrepreneur's personal contacts in both the railroad and aggregate industries. He had dealt with many of these shippers during a ten-year career with the major railroad in the region. In 1975 he had become a top administrator with the Federal Railway Administration in Washington, D.C.

Although anyone could purchase the same hopper cars as this venture (indeed, their management service revenue would come from those who did so), the entrepreneur believed that his background and personal network among aggregate shippers would combine with the state's unusual rate regulation to overcome the otherwise easy entry opportunities for railroads and other investors.

Venture G: Integrated Circuits

This 1982 startup applied its founder's knowledge of electron beam lithography to the production of integrated circuit wafers. The new manufacturing method, when perfected, would be quicker and less complicated than existing optical lithography and quicker than existing electron beam systems. The latter systems were in use at many of the largest electronics firms.

The venture used its initial funds to begin a research and development program that was intended to yield a superior emitter of electron beams. Additional efforts would be devoted to systems to focus, direct, and block the beam. The company intended to develop, fabricate, and demonstrate a prototype system. If successful, the R&D program would give the company a superior product (the beam emitter) that it could license to OEMs and end users. The company said that potential users included all current and future users of electron beam systems to manufacture integrated circuit wafers.

Venture H: Medical Diagnostic Service and Equipment

In 1981 this venture began operating a walk-in office for its new product–service: thermographic scanning to detect muscle damage, stress fractures, and other hard-to-detect internal injuries. Essentially, the company's device used infrared technology to detect the surface heat generated by such injuries. There were no rays to penetrate and threaten the body and no instruments or other devices to be introduced into the body. While the device could not determine what was wrong, it did offer positive proof that something indeed had been damaged. This was considered a great improvement over other methods or recourse to mere assertions by a patient or other sufferer.

The company purchased all components, including the vital infrared equipment and the computer software needed to analyze and interpret patient data. Several manufacturers offered such equipment, and the price had begun dropping dramatically in the past year. Assembling the equipment and establishing an office were relatively simple, inexpensive tasks.

Although the company accepted walk-in business, its major marketing objective was to develop users among the legal, medical, and insurance industries, all of whom needed reliable evidence concerning possible or alleged damage to muscles, nerves, and so forth. The company sought a reputation as an authority in such matters and was willing to provide expert witnesses to testify in court in support of the new diagnostic method and its findings.

The entrepreneur also intended to enter sports medicine, offering not only diagnostic skills but also the ability to develop and maintain a baseline data bank for each athlete on a team. Thus an athlete who complained of pain could be examined and the results contrasted to his normal state.

The founders and early investors reflected the venture's target markets. They included a director of a large insurance company, a former state commissioner of insurance, owners of professional sports teams, professional athletes, and doctors. In each instance it was believed the investors could provide credibility, contacts, and early adoptions within their domains.

Assuming the company succeeded, its founders also planned to establish mobile units to provide certain large-scale tests for schools and industrial customers.

Venture I: Microcomputer-based Process Control Systems

Beginning in December, 1978, this venture offered microcomputer-based process control systems to both end users and OEMs. The company promised custom-designed systems to solve each customer's unique problems. Although it purchased sensory components and other hardware, the company created software and microcomputers for each client. The software remained proprietary and could be modified to meet the similar needs of a subsequent customer. In addition, the company would retain the rights to add the product to its standard line.

The entrepreneur believed that his venture would avoid much of the industry's price competition because of the extensive customization embodied in its products. Customers deemed technical capability, after-sale service and support, product reliability, and speed of delivery important enough to remove many contracts from competitive bidding. Instead they frequently awarded contracts based on negotiated or estimated prices.

The company would seek to serve several process industries but intended to emphasize products for the petrochemical industry. Other customers included a commercial washing machine manufacturer, a paper producer, and a major theme park. Products would be created on a development contract basis as well as on a quoted price basis.

Venture J: Computer-aided Design and Drafting Software Systems

This venture began in 1979 with the objective of becoming a full-service supplier of CADD software. Its early operations were sustained by a development contract for a large corporation with which it shared the rights to market the software package it developed. The venture would purchase hardware, provide some on-site training, and consult for customers in order to secure software systems business. Basically, though, the company declared its intention to compete on the strength of its software, which it believed had state-of-the-art quality. This quality was cited by management as a factor that would keep customers' costs low as both hardware and software capabilities evolved.

The company intended to concentrate its efforts on developing software for the machines of one important computer maker (not IBM). In fact, the company hoped to be designated the manufacturer's *"recommended"* source of CADD software. The company also planned to develop software for use with other non-IBM computers. It described some of its planned products as having "a marketing need greater than any actual need of the majority of users."

Venture K: Christmas Tree Decorations

When a European manufacturer decided to discontinue selling its line of Christmas tree decorations in the United States., it sought someone to continue the business and to purchase raw materials from it. An executive of a U. S. manufacturer of other Christmas decorations was interested in this opportunity but could not win corporate approval of a joint venture with the Europeans. With his employer's approval and cooperation, the executive subsequently launched venture K in 1974.

The European company turned over its modest U.S. accounts and became the principal supplier of a major raw material input for venture K. The venture was competing solely in the garland and icicle segment, which accounted for about one-seventh of the domestic market for Christmas tree decorations. At the same time, the segment's leading company, about 10 times the size of the new company, exited the business and sold its icicle equipment to venture K. The venture's management described the equipment as the most efficient in the industry.

The new venture emphasized control of its inventory and finances and sought to apply more modern production planning techniques than its competitors. (Most incumbent firms were old, small, and rather traditional, according to company management.) Its marketing plans set it apart from the incumbents as venture K targeted the emerging national chains with its own sales force which maintained year-round contact with its customers. Management claimed that this was a departure from customary practice.

Management also planned to use its modern equipment and friendly supplier to pursue product innovation. Its sales force and management would work with customers to design new products when possible. This, too, would depart from standard practice in the industry, said management.

Venture L: Computer Stores

This venture was founded in 1981 to sell computer hardware, software, and "all" supplies and accessories. It also handled business forms as an authorized dealer. The founder envisioned a chain of stores catering to small businessmen. He believed that the computer industry was moving from mysterious, technology-based selling to a more conventional "straight retail approach," but that small businessmen remained troubled and afraid to make such a major purchase decision. This venture would "bridge the gap over the next three to six years" until their habits changed.

The founder described other computer retailers as "passive," waiting for buyers to come to their stores. Computer manufacturers' sales forces, on the other hand, were unable to overcome small businessmen's fears in a field setting. The solution, he reasoned, was to have "professional" sales representatives and presentation video tapes at the store and to use a wide range of external contacts to draw customers to the store for in-store programs such as conferences, consultation, receptions, and product demonstrations.

External contact would be made through in-house presentations at companies, appearances before business and professional organizations, teaching at local universities, and so on. In each setting, meeting and proselytizing small businessmen was to be the objective. The entrepreneur planned to promote both business and personal computers and related goods to these audiences.

Venture M: Electronic Games Manufacturer

This venture manufactured and sold electronic games. Its customers were game distributors who served the various establishments (for example, bars, lounges, arcades) that purchased or leased such machines. The company was founded in 1976 with the intention of offering superior games and more reliable machines. The founder believed that this would lead distributors to add his machines to the lines they already carried.

The company assembled its games from standard components that it purchased. The games were designed by staff members and by outside consultants who were used regularly. The staff and consultants also developed proprietary software for venture M's games. Neither the game designs nor the software were to be patented.

The president and the chairman of the board handled the company's sales efforts. They made direct calls on distributors and appeared at trade shows.

Venture N: Computer Sales and Services

This company was established in 1978 to sell computer hardware, software, and batch-processing services to business and professional customers. It also set up turnkey systems, provided maintenance support, and performed consulting. Its geographic market centered on a medium-sized Texas city.

Venture N's business plan did not mention any plans to specialize in particular products or services The founder formerly managed the computer center of an area vocational–technical school.

Venture O: Imported Auto Parts Store

The venture was established in 1976 to sell parts for imported automobiles. While retail sales were the principal activity of this company, a substantial minority of its sales were made at wholesale. From the beginning the founders desired to create what they called "the first chain of cloned stores" to specialize in parts for imported cars. In fact, they decided to carry parts only for Japanese automobiles and gave their business a distinctive name that clearly indicated this specialization.

Although selling some at wholesale, the founders believed they would have a higher retail percentage (and therefore a higher profit margin) than most parts stores. The largest jobbers of import parts had "fairly strong pipelines throughout the country" to independent parts stores and dealers. The founders did not plan to compete so vigorously for dealers' business but thought they could make major inroads in the retail market.

To break into the retail market the company planned to control their overhead costs by limiting their product line. They would not carry any slow-turnover items for the less common Japanese cars and trucks, although they would carry some slow-turnover items for the more popular makes. An in-store computer terminal would aid in controlling inventory.

The entrepreneur expressed his desire to franchise the store and, if possible, to sell out whenever their market appeared to be peaking.

Venture P: Ceiling Fan Manufacturer

In 1979 this venture began manufacturing ceiling fans for residential installation. The company claimed the fullness of its product line was second only to Casablanca's. Its top wholesale price was four times its lowest. The numerous models used mostly interchangeable parts; only the housing and blades differed on most models. Motors were purchased from General Electric and from a rival ceiling fan manufacturer.

The company also planned to offer lower wholesale prices than its competitors. It said it would take advantage of the low labor costs in its Sunbelt home city. To keep shipping costs low the company would sell only in the south central and southeast markets. Certain key markets would be served by a direct sales force, working on commission. The company would use distributors elsewhere. In all markets the company planned to offer frequent shipment of small orders so that customers would not have to hold large inventories. Combined with a more complete product line offering more features and styles, the low inventory requirement was expected to gain entree for venture P. The company targeted both chain stores and specialty fan stores and also expected to sell direct to homebuilders.

Venture Q: Airline

In the midst of the postderegulation turmoil of 1982, this venture sought to establish an airline. It would fly 3 long-haul routes linking a major Sunbelt city and New York–Newark, Chicago, and Los Angeles (continuing to San Francisco). It would also provide regional service from its hub to several smaller cities within a 300-mile radius.

The company planned to operate with lower costs than the long-established trunk airlines. Their costs would be lower because their employees were nonunion and lacking in seniority, their leased 737s would be operated with two instead of three pilots (as was required under union contracts), they would contract for service and support rather than maintain their own airport facilities, and they would serve the less-expensive, less-crowded, secondary airports in each major city.

The airline's fares would be lower than those of trunk carriers, but it would seek business travelers by offering a larger-than-usual percentage of first class seats and better amenities than their direct rivals in the secondary airports. Schedules would cater to business travelers, too. Interlining would be available with other airlines serving the same airports, but not with the trunk lines that used only the principal airports.

The company's prestartup business plan emphasized its lower costs, business-oriented scheduling, and upgraded first-class service. It also mentioned the possibility of eventual geographic expansion to most of the United States if the company proved successful.

Bibliography

Abell, Derek F. 1980. *Defining the Business: The Starting Point of Strategic Planning.* Englewood Cliffs, N.J.: Prentice-Hall.

Allen, Louis L. 1968. *Starting and Succeeding in Your Own Small Business.* New York: Grosset & Dunlap.

Altman, Edward I. 1968. "Financial Ratios, Discriminant Analysis and the Prediction of Corporate Bankruptcy." *Journal of Finance* 23 (September):589–609.

American Scientific Enterprise, Inc. 1980. *Startup Business—The Offensive Side of the Game.* Great Neck, N.Y.: American Scientific Enterprise.

Anderson, Carl R., and Carl P. Zeithaml. 1984. "Stage of the Product Life Cycle, Business Strategy, and Business Performance." *Academy of Management Journal* 27:5–24.

Beaver, W. H. 1966. "Financial Ratios as Predictors of Failure." in *Empirical Research in Accounting: Selected Studies,* supplement to *Journal of Accounting Research* 4 (Spring):71–111.

Beste, Frederick J. III. 1982. "Community Development Corporations and Economic Development Commissions." In *How to Raise Venture Capital,* edited by Stanley E. Pratt. New York: Charles Scribner's Sons, pp. 63–71.

Bettis, Richard A. 1983. "Modern Financial Theory, Corporate Strategy, and Public Policy: Three Conundrums." *Academy of Management Review* 8:406–415.

Biggadike, E. Ralph. 1979*a*. *Corporate Diversification: Entry, Strategy, and Performance.* Boston: Division of Research, Graduate School of Business Administration, Harvard University.

———1979*b*. "The Risky Business of Diversification." *Harvard Business Review* 57 (May–June):103–111.

Brockhaus, Robert H. 1975. "I–E Locus of Control Scores as Predictors of Entrepreneurial Intentions." Paper presented at the annual meeting of the Academy of Management, New Orleans.

———1980*a*. "Psychological and Environmental Factors Which Distinguish the Successful from the Unsuccessful Entrepreneur: A Longitudinal Study." *Proceedings, Academy of Management*, pp. 368–372.

———1980*b*. "Psychology of the Entrepreneur." Paper presented at the Conference on Research and Education in Entrepreneurship, St. Louis University, March 24–25.

———1980*c*. "Risk-Taking Propensity of Entrepreneurs." *Academy of Management Journal* 23:509–520.

Brockhaus, Robert H., and W. R. Nord. 1979. "An Exploration of the Factors Affecting the Entrepreneurial Decision: Personal Characteristics vs. Environmental Conditions." *Proceedings, Academy of Management*, pp. 364–368.

Bruno, Albert V., and Tyzoon T. Tyebjee. 1983. "The One that Got Away: A Study of Ventures Rejected by Venture Capitalists." In *Frontiers of Entrepreneurship Research, 1983*, John A. Hornaday, Jeffry A. Timmons, and Karl H. Vesper. Proceedings of the 1983 Conference on Entrepreneurship. Wellesley, Mass: Babson College, pp. 289–306.

Buchele, Robert. 1967. *Business Policy in Growing Firms*. Scranton, Pa.: Chandler Publishing Company.

Burgelman, Robert A. 1980. "Managing Innovating Systems: A Study of the Process of Internal Corporate Ventures." Ph.D. diss., Columbia University, New York.

Carland, James W., Frank Hoy, William R. Boulton, and Jo Ann C. Carland. 1984. "Differentiating Entrepreneurs from Small Business Owners: A Conceptualization." *Academy of Management Review* 9:354–359.

Caves, Richard E., and Thomas A. Pugel. 1980. *Intraindustry Differences in Conduct and Performance: Viable Strategies in U. S. Manufacturing Industries*. Monograph series in Finance and Economics, Monograph 1980-2, Graduate School of Business Administration, Salomon Brothers Center for the Study of Financial Institutions, New York University.

Collins, Orvis F., and David G. Moore. 1964. *The Enterprising Man* (MSU Business Studies, 1964; Bureau of Business and Economic Research; Graduate School of Business Administration; Michigan State University). East Lansing, Mich.: Michigan State University.

Cooper, Arnold C. 1971. *The Founding of Technology-based Firms*. Milwaukee, Wis.: The Center for Venture Management.

———1979. "Strategic Management: New Ventures and Small Business." in *Strategic Management*, edited by Dan E. Schendel and Charles W. Hofer. Boston: Little, Brown, pp. 316–327.

Cooper, Arnold C., and Albert Bruno. 1977. "Success Among High-Technology Firms." *Business Horizons* 20 (April):16–22.

Cooper, Arnold C., and William C. Dunkelberg. 1981. "Influences Upon Entrepreneurship—A Large-Scale Study." Paper presented at the Academy of Management meeting, San Diego.

Dess, Gregory G., and Peter S. Davis, 1984. "Porter's (1980) Generic Strategies as Determinants of Strategic Group Membership and Organizational Performance." *Academy of Management Journal* 27:467–488.

Dingee, Alexander L. M., Jr., Leonard E. Smollen, and Brian Haslett. 1982. "Characteristics of a Successful Entrepreneur." In *How to Raise Venture Capital,* edited by Stanley E. Pratt. New York: Charles Scribner's Sons, pp. 15–26.

Dominguez, John R. 1974. *Venture Capital*. Lexington Mass.: D. C. Heath.

Dorsey, Terry. 1979. *Operating Guidelines for Effective Venture Capital Funds Management*. Technical Series, No. 3. Austin, Tex.: The Institute for Constructive Capitalism, University of Texas.

Douglass, Merrill E. 1976. "Relating Education to Entrepreneurial Success." *Business*

Horizons 19 (December):410–44.

Fast, Norman D. 1978. *The Rise and Fall of Corporate New Venture Divisions*. Ann Arbor, Mich.: UMI Research Press.

———1982. "Venture Capital Investment and Technology Development." in *Frontiers of Entrepreneurship Research*, edited by Karl H. Vesper. Wellesley, Mass.: Babson College Center for Entrepreneurial Studies, pp. 288–293.

Fleischer, Michele H. 1985. "The Venture Capital 100: Caution is the Word." *Venture* 7 (June):48–56.

Gartner, William. 1983. "Entry Strategies in an Emerging Industry." *Proceedings, Academy of Management*, pp. 413–416.

Gregg, Gail. 1984. "Investing in Entrepreneurs." *Venture* 6 (June):46–50.

Gupta, Anil K. 1984. "Contingency Linkages Between Strategy and General Manager Characteristics: A Conceptual Examination." *Academy of Management Review* 9 (July):399–412.

Gupta, Udayan. 1983. "SBICs." *Venture* 5 (October):66–68.

Hall, William K. 1980. "Survival Strategies in a Hostile Environment." *Harvard Business Review* 58 (September–October):75–85.

Hambrick, Donald C., Ian C. MacMillan, and Diana L. Day. 1982. "Strategic Attributes and Performance in the BCG Matrix—A PIMS-Based Analysis of Industrial Product Businesses." *Academy of Management Journal* 25:510–531.

Hamermesh, Richard G., M. J. Anderson, Jr., and M. E. Harris. 1978. "Strategies for Low Market Share Businesses." *Harvard Business Review* 56 (May–June):95–102.

Harrigan, Kathryn Rudie. 1980*a*. *Strategies for Declining Businesses*. Lexington, Mass.: Lexington Books.

———1980*b*. "Strategies for Declining Industries." *Journal of Business Strategy* 1 (Fall):20–34.

———1981. "Deterrents to Divestiture." *Academy of Management Journal* 24:306–323.

———1983*a*. "Research Methodologies for Contingency Approaches to Business Strategy." *Academy of Management Review* 8:398–405.

———1983*b*. *Strategies for Vertical Integration*. Lexington, Mass.: Lexington Books.

Hatten, Kenneth J. 1974. "Strategic Models in the Brewing Industry." Ph.D. diss., Purdue University, West Lafayette, Ind.

Hill, Richard M. and James D. Hlavacek. 1977. "Learning from Failure: Ten Guidelines for Venture Management." *California Management Review* 19 (Summer):5–16.

Hoad, William M, and Peter Rosko. 1964. *Management Factors Contributing to the Success and Failure of New Small Manufacturers*. Ann Arbor, Mich.: Bureau of Business Research, University of Michigan.

Hofer, Charles W. 1975. "Toward a Contingency Theory of Business Strategy." *Academy of Management Journal* 18:784–810.

———1977. "Conceptual Constructs for Formulating Corporate and Business Strategies." Boston: Intercollegiate Case Clearing House.

———1980. "Turnaround Strategies." *Journal of Business Strategy* 1 (Summer):19–31.

———1981. "Product-Market Fundamentals vs. the Product Life Cycle." Paper presented at the Conference on Nontraditional Approaches to Policy Research, University of Southern California, November.

Hofer, Charles W., and Dan E. Schendel. 1978. *Strategy Formulation: Analytical Concepts*. St. Paul, Minn.: West Publishing Co.

Hornaday, John A., and John Aboud. 1971. "Characteristics of Successful Entrepreneurs." *Personnel Psychology* 24 (Summer):141–153.

Johnson, James M. 1979. "Determinants of Unsuccessful Risk Capital Funding by Small Business." *American Journal of Small Business* 4 (July):31–38.

Kirzner, Israel M. 1979. *Perception, Opportunity, and Profit*. Chicago: University of Chicago Press.

Knight, Frank H. 1921. *Risk, Uncertainty and Profit*. New York: Houghton Mifflin.

Komives, John L. 1972. "A Preliminary Study of the Personal Values of High Technology Entrepreneurs." In *Technical Entrepreneurship: A Symposium*, Milwaukee, Wis.: The Center for Venture Management.

Kravitz, Lee. 1984. "The Venture Capital 100." *Venture* 6 (June):60–68.

Lamont, Lawrence M. 1972. "What Entrepreneurs Learn from Experience." *Journal of Small Business Management* 10 (July):36–41.

Larson, Carl M., and Ronald C. Clute. 1974. "The Failure Syndrome." *American Journal of Small Business* 4 (October):35–43.

Levine, Jon. 1982. "The Venture Capital 100: Once Again, It's a Buyer's Market." *Venture* (June):80–90.

Liles, Patrick R. 1974. *New Business and the Entrepreneur*. Homewood, Ill.: Richard D. Irwin.

Litwin, George H., and Robert A. Stringer. 1968. *Motivation and Organizational Climate*. Boston: Division of Research, Graduate School of Business Administration, Harvard University.

Loftin, Richard. 1981. "What Capitalists Want." *Inc.* (November):144–147.

MacMillan, Ian C., Donald C. Hambrick, and Diana L. Day. 1982. "The Product Portfolio and Profitability—A PIMS-Based Analysis of Industrial-Product Businesses." *Academy of Management Journal* 25:733–755.

Madlin, Nancy. 1985. "The Venture Survey: Sticking to Business Plans." *Venture* 7 (April):25.

Mancuso, Joseph. 1974. "The Entrepreneur's Quiz." In *The Entrepreneur's Handbook 2*, edited by Joseph Mancuso. Dedham, Mass.: Artech House, pp. 235–239.

Marascuilo, Leonard A., and Maryellen McSweeney. 1977. *Nonparametric and Distribution-Free Methods for the Social Sciences*. Monterey, Calif.: Brooks/Cole Publishing Company.

Martin, Dolores Tremewan. 1979. "Alternative Views of Mengerian Entrepreneurship." *History of Political Economy* 11:271–285.

McClelland, David. 1961. *The Achieving Society*. Princeton, N. J.: D. Van Nostrand.

McClelland, David C. 1965. "N Achievement and Entrepreneurship: A Longitudinal Study ." *Journal of Personality and Social Psychology* 1:389–392.

McClelland, David C., and David G. Winter. 1969. *Motivating Economic Achievement*. New York: Free Press.

Menger, Carl. 1981. *Principles of Economics*. Translated by James Dingwall and Bert F. Hoselitz from *Grundsatze der Volkswirtschaftslehre*, 1871. New York: New York University Press.

Mescon, Timothy Scott. 1979. "Entrepreneurship in the Real Estate Industry: A Comparative Analysis of Independent and Franchise Brokers." Ph.D. diss., The University of Georgia, Athens, Ga.

Mises, Ludwig von. 1966. *Human Action*. 3rd rev. ed. Chicago: Henry Regnery Company.

Mitroff, Ian I., and Richard O. Mason. 1982. "Business Policy and Metaphysics: Some Philosophical Considerations." *Academy of Management Review* 7:361–371.

Patel, Pater, and Michael Younger. 1978. "A Frame of Reference for Strategy Development." *Long-Range Planning* 11 (April):6–12.

Penrose, Edith Tilton. 1959. *The Theory of the Growth of the Firm*. New York: John Wiley & Sons.

Porter, Michael E. 1980. *Competitive Strategy*. New York: Free Press.

———1981. "The Contributions of Industrial Organization to Strategic Management." *Academy of Management Review* 6:609–620.

Power, Daniel J., and George P. Huber. 1982. "Guidelines for Using Key Informants and Retrospective Reports in Strategic Management Research." In *Proceedings of the 14th Annual Meeting of the American Institute of Decision Sciences*. edited by Gregory P. White, San Francisco: American Institute of Decision Sciences. pp. 29–31.

Prescott, John E. 1981. "The Development of an Industry Typology." Paper presented at the Academy of Management meeting, San Diego.

Rink, David R., and John E. Swan. 1979. "Product Life Cycle Research: A Literature Review." *Journal of Business Research* 7:219–242.

Roberts, Edward B. 1968. "A Basic Study of Innovators; How to Keep and Capitalize on Their Talents." *Research Management* 11 (July):249–266.

———1970. "How to Succeed in a New Technology Enterprise." *Technology Review* 73 (December):25.

Rotter, J. B. 1966. "Generalized Expectancies for Internal Versus External Control of Reinforcement." *Psychological Monographs: General and Applied,* 80, no. 1, Whole No.609.

Rumelt, Richard. 1979. "Evaluation of Strategy: Theory and Models." in *Strategic Management,* edited by Dan E. Schendel and Charles W. Hofer. Boston: Little, Brown, pp. 196–212.

Sandberg, William R. 1984. "The Determinants of New Venture Performance: Strategy, Industry Structure and Entrepreneur." Ph.D. diss., University of Georgia, Athens, Ga.

Sandberg, William R., and Charles W. Hofer. 1982. "A Strategic Management Perspective on the Determinants of New Venture Success." in *Frontiers of Entrepreneurship Research,* edited by Karl H. Vesper. Wellesley, Mass.: Babson Center for Entrepreneurial Studies, pp. 204–237.

Schendel, Dan E., and Charles W. Hofer, eds. 1979. *Strategic Management*. Boston: Little, Brown.

Scherer, F. M. 1970. *Industrial Market Structure and Economic Performance*. Chicago: Rand McNally.

Schrage, Harry. 1965. "The R&D Entrepreneur: Profile of Success." *Harvard Business Review* 43 (November):56–69.

Schumpeter, Joseph A. 1934. *The Theory of Economic Development*. Cambridge,

Mass.: Harvard University Press.

Sexton, Donald L. 1980. "Characteristics and Role Demands of Successful Entrepreneurs." Paper presented at the annual meeting of the Academy of Management, Detroit.

Shapero, Albert. 1975. "The Displaced, Uncomfortable Entrepreneur." *Psychology Today* (November):83–89.

———1980. "Some Social Dimensions of Entrepreneurship." Paper presented at the Conference on Research and Education in Entrepreneurship, Baylor University, Waco, Tex.

———1981. "Numbers That Lie." *Inc.* 3 (May):16–18.

Sharma, Subhash, and Vijay Mahajan. 1980. "Early Warning Indicators of Business Failure." *Journal of Marketing* 44 (Fall):80–89.

Siegel, Sidney. 1956. *Nonparametric Statistics for the Behavioral Sciences*. New York: McGraw-Hill.

Silver, A. David. 1978. *Characteristics of Successful Entrepreneurs*. New York: The Comptere Group.

Smith, Norman Raymond. 1967. *The Entrepreneur and His Firm: The Relationship Between Type of Man and Type of Company*. East Lansing, Mich.: Bureau of Business and Economic Research, Graduate School of Business Administration, Michigan State University.

Soukup, William R. 1979. "Strategic Responses to Technological Threats." Ph.D. diss., Purdue University, West Lafayette, Ind.

South, Stephen E. 1981. "Competitive Advantages: The Cornerstone of Strategic Thinking." *Journal of Business Strategy* 1 (Spring):15–25.

Stahl, Michael J., and Thomas W. Zimmerer. 1984. "Modeling Strategic Acquisition Decisions: A Simulation of Executives' Acquisition Decisions." *Academy of Management Journal* 27 (June):369–383.

Stiff, Ronald, and Inder Khera. 1981. "Strategies for Low Market-Share Companies." *Applied Business and Administration Quarterly* 1 (Spring):8–12.

Susbauer, Jeffrey. 1979. "Commentary." In *Strategic Management,* edited by Dan E. Schendel and Charles W. Hofer. Boston: Little, Brown, pp. 327–332.

Szilagyi, Andrew D., and David M. Schweiger. 1984. "Matching Managers to Strategies: A Review and Suggested Framework." *Academy of Management Review* 9 (October):626–637.

Timmons, Jeffry A. 1971. "Black is Beautiful—Is It Bountiful?" *Harvard Business Review* 49 (November):81–94.

———1973. "Motivating Economic Achievement: A Five Year Appraisal." *Proceedings of the 5th Annual Meeting of the American Institute of Decision Sciences,* edited by Manfred W. Hopfe. Boston, Mass, pp. 220–223.

———1982. "Venture Capital in Sweden." In *Frontiers of Entrepreneurship Research,* edited by Karl H. Vesper. Wellesley, Mass.: Babson College Center for Entrepreneurial Studies, pp. 294–312.

Tyebjee, Tyzoon T., and Albert V. Bruno. 1984. "A Model of Venture Capitalist Investment Activity." *Management Science* 30:1051–1066.

Vesper, Karl H. 1979. "Commentary." In *Strategic Management,* edited by Dan E. Schendel and Charles W. Hofer. Boston: Little, Brown, pp. 332–338.

———1980. *New Venture Strategies*. Englewood Cliffs, N. J.: Prentice-Hall.

———1983. *Entrepreneurship and National Policy.* Chicago: Heller Institute for Small Business Policy Papers.

Wainer, Herbert A., and Irwin M. Rubin. 1969. "Motivation of Research and Development Entrepreneurs." *Journal of Applied Psychology* 53:178–184.

Wasson, Chester. 1974. *Dynamic Competitive Strategy and Product Life Cycles.* St. Charles, Ill.: Challenge Books.

Webster, Frederick Arthur. 1977. "Entrepreneurs and Ventures: An Attempt at Classification and Clarification." *Academy of Management Review* 2:54–61.

White, Richard. 1977. *The Entrepreneur's Manual.* Radnor, Pa.: Chilton.

Woo, Carolyn Y. Y. 1980. "Strategies for Low Market Share Businesses." Ph.D. diss., Purdue University, West Lafayette, Ind.

Woo, Carolyn Y. Y., and Arnold C. Cooper. 1981. "Strategies of Effective Low Share Businesses." *Strategic Management Journal* 2 (October–December):301–318.

Yip, George S. 1982. *Barriers to Entry: A Corporate-Strategy Perspective.* Lexington, Mass.: Lexington Books.

Zaleznik, Abraham, and Manfred F. R. Kets de Vries. 1976. "What Makes Entrepreneurs Entrepreneurial?" *Business and Society Review* 17 (Spring):18–23.

Index

About the Author

William R. Sandberg (Ph.D., Georgia; M.B.A., B.S., Northwestern) is an assistant professor of strategic management at the University of Houston. His research interests include new venture strategies and performance, venture capitalism, industry analysis, and strategic decision-making techniques.

Professor Sandberg received the 1985 Heizer Award for Outstanding Research in the Field of New Venture Development, presented by the Business Policy and Planning Division of the Academy of Management for his study of the determinants of new venture performance. He is an author of articles in the *Academy of Management Journal* and the *Academy of Management Review* and of papers in the *Proceedings* of the Academy of Management and the Babson College Conference on Entrepreneurship.